LEADERSHIP RISING

Raise Your Awareness
Raise Your Leadership
Raise Your Life

JOHN ANTAL

CASEMATE

Philadelphia & Oxford

Published in the United States of America and Great Britain in 2021 by
CASEMATE PUBLISHERS
1950 Lawrence Road, Havertown, PA 19083, USA
and
The Old Music Hall, 106–108 Cowley Road, Oxford OX4 1JE, UK

Paperback Edition: ISBN 978-1-63624-066-4
Digital Edition: ISBN 978-1-63624-067-1

A CIP record for this book is available from the British Library

Printed and bound in the United States by Integrated Books International

For a complete list of Casemate titles, please contact:

CASEMATE PUBLISHERS (US)
Telephone (610) 853-9131
Fax (610) 853-9146
Email: casemate@casematepublishers.com
www.casematepublishers.com

CASEMATE PUBLISHERS (UK)
Telephone (01865) 241249
Email: casemate-uk@casematepublishers.co.uk
www.casematepublishers.co.uk

Contents

Acknowledgements   v
Preface: Read to Lead   ix

1   Know Yourself   1
2   Determine Your Purpose   31
3   Visualize Your Leadership Compass   57
4   A Personal Definition of Leadership   85
5   Develop Your Leadership Superpowers   99
6   Shape Your Destiny by Learning How to Decide   121
7   Rally Points for Challenging Times   153

Bibliography   169
Index   171
About the Author   176

Acknowledgements

Every book is the work of many people. I wish to thank those who helped transform *Leadership Rising* from a thought to publication. First, I want to thank my wife, Uncha Antal. She is the fuel for my fire and the love of my life. With her, anything is possible. Second, I want to thank my good friends, Francis Fierko and Rick Jung, for their counsel, wisdom, and superb editing. Fran is as amazing a leader as he is an expert editor, and his efforts in helping with the manuscript were decisive. Rick was also central to the transformation of the work from draft to final version, reading every word and illuminating my shortfalls. I also want to thank the many people who took time to read, comment, and offer advice to me on how to improve the preliminary versions that I circulated prior to the final draft. These include, in alphabetical order, James and Beth Antal, Edward Braese, Ray Dishaw, Shawn Graves, and Carolyn Petracca. Finally, I am thankful for the editing and advice from Ruth Sheppard, Alison Griffiths, Megan Yates and the entire team at Casemate Publishers. I am profoundly grateful to you all.

Raise your awareness.
Raise your leadership.
Raise your life.

Preface

Read to Lead

My purpose is to develop leaders and inspire service. Purpose is the basis for all motivation. Without purpose, your goals lack direction. Without leaders of purpose, teams cannot reach their destinations. If you live your life with purpose, your actions move you towards a definitive goal. With purpose, you can move forward, explore, and grow. My purpose for writing *Leadership Rising* is to empower you to raise your leadership awareness to become a winning leader.

Leadership is of vital importance to you, or you would not have selected this book. Leaders change the potential energy of a group into the kinetic energy of a team. If you win at leading, you can win at life.

Navigating your leadership journey can be difficult. To navigate, first you must determine where you are. If you do not know where you are, then you are lost. Next, you must decide which direction to go. If you start by heading the wrong way, you waste precious time and energy and may find yourself traveling in circles, getting nowhere. By starting in the right direction, you save time and energy. In addition, you gain a tremendous advantage over those who do not know the way. Finally, you must know where you want to go. Traveling without a destination is pointless.

Today, to navigate and move from one physical location to another, you use the technology of the Global Positioning Satellite (GPS) network on your smartphone. This makes navigation effortless as, after you input a destination, the GPS marks your location on a detailed map and gives you voice-prompted, point-by-point directions. Your leadership journey is a different matter. There is no GPS to help you navigate the leadership terrain. No technology can replace leadership. Leading requires you to deliver a holistic, human effort all day, every day, in calm and in crisis. To learn to lead, you must chart your course across this turbulent territory in more traditional ways, by first developing a mental map of the journey and then developing your own internal compass. Your compass needle points true when you are following your purpose and your values. Together, these provide your leadership with location, direction, and destination.

Leadership is the paramount ingredient that inspires people to cooperate and accomplish goals. If your leadership level is low, your life will be hard as it will be difficult to motivate people to work with you. If your leadership level is high, you can influence people to accomplish specific goals. Often, the best leaders inspire their teams to achieve seemingly impossible objectives. Accomplishing what was considered unobtainable is the magic of great leadership. Leadership, however, is not magic. You do not achieve great deeds at the snap of your fingers. As in the development of any worthwhile skill, sharpening your leadership takes study, practice, and discipline. The discipline of leadership requires persistent action to attain an intended result. Discipline earns the deed. Just like doing push-ups, the more you exercise each day, the stronger you become and therefore the more push-ups you can do. This book provides the mental push-ups that will raise your leadership awareness.

Leadership is not a title or position and comes in many forms. Anyone with a driving desire and the basic cognitive ability can rise to lead. Leadership can come from the newest member of the team or from the most experienced. The best leaders are effective communicators, but there were prominent leaders in history who could not read. Conversely, there have been abysmal bosses who were as articulate as Shakespeare but incompetent as leaders. By raising your awareness of leadership, you can learn the difference.

Leadership involves influencing people. There is no simple equation for leadership, and no formula to mass-produce leaders. The leadership journey is a personal effort of introspection, education, experience, and most importantly, dedication. There are as many types of people, teams, groups, and organizations as there are stars in the night sky, but you can raise your awareness and learn to lead others if you have the will to engage and improve your character, competencies and commitment. No matter what your situation, age, or circumstance, what defines you is how you rise, grow, and lead. You can raise your leadership, increase your chances for success, and improve the lives of those who follow you. If you are not growing your leadership, it is withering. Eventually it dies. There are few things sadder than an experienced leader whose map is out of date and whose compass no longer points true. Leadership, therefore, is a subject to ponder and refresh at all stages of your life.

In seven short chapters, this book will rapidly raise your awareness of leadership. Outstanding leaders know the value of time. Once a minute is past, we lose it forever. Time is a finite asset that cannot be stored. Time is not just money; time is the measure of everything. There are 24 hours in a day, but few people make the most of those hours. To squander time is to waste life. To win time, therefore, is to win life. As a leader, to misuse other people's time not only wastes their hours, but also their lives, as we measure life in hours, days, and years. "Time is the most precious element of human existence," writes Denis Waitley, author and national authority on high-level performance and personal development. "The successful person knows how to put energy into time and how to draw success from time." Through successful actions, you can win time for yourself, those you lead, and those who benefit from what you deliver or produce.

Leadership Rising describes leadership as a human art and not a science, as there is no equation or step-by-step process that can mass produce leaders. Being a capable artist requires a unique skill set and the discipline to master those skills. Leadership is a developed skill. It is difficult to replicate leadership even in the best environments and some of the best leadership schools have produced poor leaders. Because it is an art, it must be learned, experienced, and practiced. No one is born a leader, and although some are graced with innate advantages, leaders are ultimately self-made. In addition, the leadership environment is ever-changing. Leadership effective in one setting may not work in another. Every leadership interaction has many outcomes as it involves human interaction with people who have free will. If you treat people like "replacement parts" and apply the same leadership recipe over and over again, you demonstrate that you do not know how to lead. You must adapt to every new leadership challenge. All teams are different, every group comprises unique individuals, and most situations are distinct. Without the internal and consistent drive to improve character, competencies and commitment, your leadership stagnates. Your compass is pointing true, you may be on the right azimuth, but you will need to create a new map for each unique situation. Leadership involves the discipline of consistently taking the right actions, for the right reasons, for both you and for those you lead.

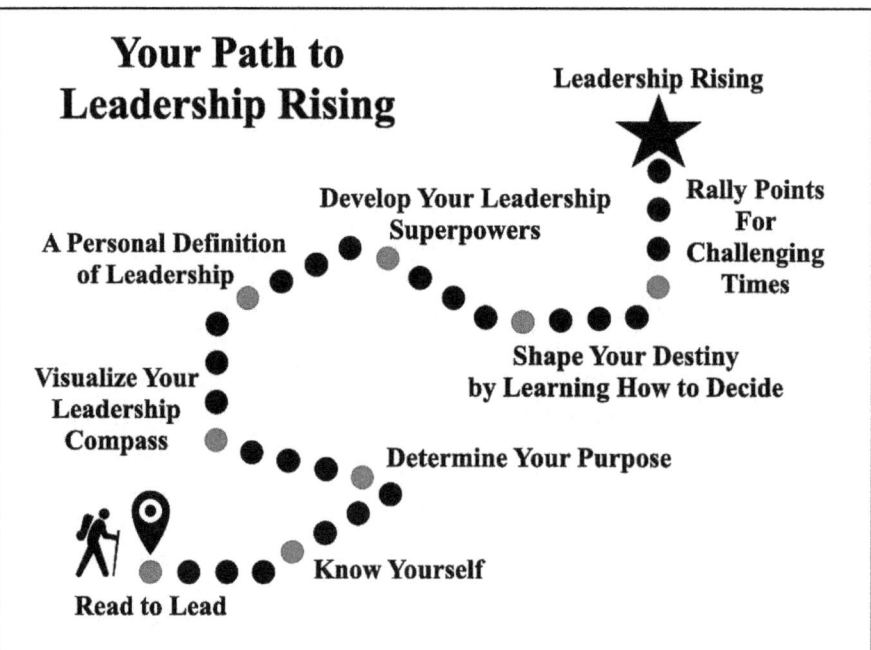

Throughout this book, you will identify, gauge and develop methods to improve your leadership. The focus of the first chapter, "Know Yourself," is to inspire you to reflect on who you are and to critically examine yourself. Knowing, and then being yourself, is harder than you think, as it requires a clear and honest assessment of your weaknesses and strengths. Chapter Two, "Determine Your Purpose," will focus you on determining this seminal objective. This may seem a daunting task, but it is only impossible if you never try. The choices you make each day either move you toward fulfilling your purpose, or not. If you want your choices to have meaning, know your purpose. Chapter Three, "Visualize Your Leadership Compass," challenges you to view leadership in your mind's eye and create a model to guide your thinking. The best leaders develop visualization as a basic skill, and you can learn to do this. In Chapter Four, "A Personal Definition of Leadership," you will articulate your understanding of leadership by crafting a personal definition that is both convincing and descriptive. You have heard the saying: "talk the talk and walk the walk." You must support what you say, not just with words, but with actions. If you cannot tell people how you personally define leadership, how can you hope to exercise your vision and purpose to lead others? The fifth chapter, "Develop your Leadership Superpowers," requires introspection and analysis to discover your innate skills to unlock your personal "superpowers." You may not recognize it, but you possess superpowers that can electrify and enhance your leadership abilities. All of us can unleash at least one superpower.

Chapter Six, "Shape your Destiny by Learning How to Decide," challenges you to review how you decide. Leaders decide. The quality and timeliness of your decisions often determine your team's success or failure. Few people will follow a loser for very long. They expect their leaders to win and magnify their efforts, not waste them. No one wants to follow you if you fail to make a decision, or consistently make poor ones. The seventh chapter, "Rally Points for Challenging Times," summarizes our discussion of leadership with a list of "rally points" that can make the difference between your success or failure as a leader. A leadership rally point is a mental trigger to focus the leader's principles, character, competencies and commitment toward a purpose. Understand these rally points and they will arm you with winning advice. The best leaders borrow or develop rally points along the path of their leadership journey. Whether you adopt or adapt these guidelines for your particular purpose, or develop your own, is inconsequential. What matters is that you have a personal leadership map and compass that direct you to critical rally points which will guide you on your journey of raising your leadership awareness and abilities.

If you are an emerging leader, this book will provide you with a mind map and internal compass to maintain a bearing during your leadership journey. Your mind map will outline the contours of the leadership topography, the compass you create in your heart and your mind will provide direction, and your purpose generates a destination. As you gain more experience, you will add to the map, enhancing your knowledge of the leadership environment and filling in any gaps. As you continue to earn experience as a leader, you will build more confidence in following your compass and you will learn if it points true or not. If it does, follow it. If it does not, realign it. You calibrate your compass when you differentiate between right and wrong. You ignore this at your peril.

If you are an experienced leader, this book is also for you. You will find in the following pages reinforcement, confirmation, and a series of knowledge points to add to your existing cognitive map and compass. As an experienced leader you understand the need to read to lead. You are a lifelong learner and always looking for ways to better coach, teach and mentor yourself and others. As an experienced leader, you will find this book useful to develop other leaders at every level of skill and awareness and at every chance you get. Experienced leaders have a responsibility to develop and grow the next generation of leaders. When you grow leaders in your organization, people notice, and they will see that you are a leader who cultivates other leaders. They will want to work with you as they know they will learn and grow under your mentorship.

Our world is ever-changing, and the pace of change is accelerating. The very nature of work, leadership, and what it means to be human, will transform in the days ahead. In the past, leadership was the one constant in the cascading evolution of humanity. Where there was no leadership, the people perished. Where there was effective leadership, they flourished. Teams without effective leadership failed. Individuals or groups can provide leadership, but if it does not exist, there is little movement forward, and often, chaos reigns. Maximize your impact in life for the good by continuing to rise to leadership challenges and learn. Learning to lead is hard, but it is vital. In an era of dynamic change, our world needs effective leaders more than ever before.

You can improve your leadership by raising your awareness. Awareness involves comprehension of the leadership environment and events in relation to time and resources, the perception of their meaning, and the projection of their future state. Since leadership is dynamic, the future state is ever-changing. What you did yesterday is yesterday's news. How well you are leading today is a test of your effectiveness. How capably you meet tomorrow's challenges is the measure of your influence. The legacy of your personal story is how you lead and rise to the challenges of life. The best leaders engage in a discipline of lifelong learning to improve their leadership skills. They strive to be a "learn-it-all," not a "know-it-all." They understand that leaders must READ to LEAD. Reading is an exercise to strengthen your intellect. The more you read about leadership, the greater your awareness. The more aware you are, the more likely you are to act correctly. The best leaders adopt the discipline of lifelong reading and learning.

You decide how high your leadership rises. It does not matter how experienced, or inexperienced, a leader you are. Study, definition, and reflection benefit every leader. Outstanding leaders continuously develop better definitions to generate understanding. They consistently strive to reflect to know themselves. They persistently visualize how to lead and communicate more effectively. They learn from each failure and every success, and never let failure stop them. Along this journey, they improve their ability to motivate people and sharpen their skills to make timely, winning decisions. I trust that this book will raise your awareness, raise your leadership, and raise your life. Use this recognition to benefit yourself, your family, team or business, your community and country, and the common good.

John Antal

Self-Assessment

Master Self

Find your "Why"

Know

Path Follower

LEADERSHIP

Pathfinder

Crucibles

Reflect

Process

Be Yourself

Outcome

CHAPTER I

Know Yourself

The First Step

Forget fear. Forget pain. Keep going. The pathfinder pushed on, guiding the team into uncharted territory: wild, hazardous, and unknown. Snow covered the mountains. Some men shivered from the cold. Were they lost? Would they survive? What if there was no way through the mountains? Several scouts had searched for a pass, and nearly all had failed. All except one, and that man was the pathfinder at the front of the column. The team had followed their leader for 10 weeks across wild and dangerous country to arrive at this steep rise. A few men had died along the way. Carrying heavy packs and axes, the men labored for each breath as they struggled up the slope. They were at the end of their strength and about to give up.

"Keep going," the pathfinder shouted from the front of the column. "Forward, just a bit more. The gap is close. Keep moving." Struggling over snow and ice, the foot-sore column marched forward. The pathfinder knew where to go, breaking through thickets of branches, marking trees to cut, and winding around boulders. The column stopped as pine trees as thick as a castle's wall blocked their path. Without hesitation, the pathfinder took out his ax and began chopping. Other men unpacked their tools and began to work. With sharp axes they felled the trees, the path opened, and the men tramped on. As the trail narrowed, the pathfinder designated dangerous spots for the others to avoid along the way. After an arduous climb, they reached the top. Behind them was a clear path that others could follow. In front of them lay their goal. The group paused, catching their breath, and took in the amazing view. The lush land below appeared in great majesty as the golden, warm rays of the sun bore down upon them. Their eyes gazed upon a magnificent scene, a valley that appeared like a green poem in motion, with a line of pine trees along a wide stream. The men knew they were seeing something that few others had ever seen before. The leader pointed to the center of the valley.

"That's our rally point. Let's go. Follow me."

This is a true story of a journey of exploration that occurred in March 1775, only a few months before the "shot heard round the world" was fired at Lexington, Massachusetts, igniting the American Revolution. Sixteen months later, America declared its independence from Great Britain and became a new nation. The tall, tough, and humble man who led the group of pioneers into this unknown land was Daniel Boone. Together, his team cut a path and found a notch through the steep Allegheny Mountains. The Alleghenies had been a barrier to westward settlements. Only a few pathfinders knew the way. Someone had to lead the way for others to follow, and Daniel was that man. The trail was steep, rough and narrow, and they would never have succeeded in the journey without someone who had learned the path, walked the path, visualized and communicated the goal, and then guided them to the destination: the fertile farmlands and abundant hunting forests of Kentucky.

Daniel Boone led the expedition of 31 ax-men in March 1775 to clear a path that became known as the Wilderness Trail. According to Stewart Edward White, in his classic book *Daniel Boone Wilderness Scout*:

> It was at first, as these men made it, merely a trail, fit only for packhorses; but its grades, the selection of its route through the passes and over the rough country is a testimony to Boone's practical eye and engineering knowledge. With great skill he took advantage of buffalo roads, Indian traces, his own hunter's trail, and the Warrior Path of the Indians, connecting them up, cutting through the forests and dense canebrakes, blazing mile trees for distance.

In April 1775, his party of frontiersmen finished building a fort that became the first American settlement in Kentucky. Christened Fort Boonesborough, in honor of Daniel's leadership, the fort eventually grew into a settlement. The development of the Wilderness Trail is an amazing turning point in American history that broke new ground and opened up exciting possibilities. Boonesborough soon became a waypoint for more pioneers, and 221,000 Americans eventually settled in Kentucky by 1800. Daniel's saga is the age-old story of leadership, where the leader learns how to guide and inspire others to achieve more than they think they can. Today, you too can be a pathfinder who brings people to places they have never been before and leads them to achieve magnificent things that they never thought that they could accomplish.

Fast forward to the 21st century. In February 2013, a maverick entrepreneur is in a crisis. He has promised to deliver a cutting-edge product but does not have the cash-flow to pay his workers. To stave off insolvency, he assembles every employee and explains the situation. Customers have promised to buy, but now he must ask them to buy in advance of receipt of the product. He tells his team that no matter what they were currently doing, their new job is to convince customers to pay up front and send in their money. He also announces that he will guarantee the resale price of the product, in writing, with his personal funds, to give every customer faith in the transaction. Secretly, as a worst-case option, he goes to a major technology company and asks if they would buy his enterprise to keep his employees on salary and the plant in operation. During these negotiations, a miracle occurs, one that his leadership inspired. Every worker, no matter what their previous job, focuses on closing deals. With the new promise of a guaranteed resale price, they close enough contracts to make the company profitable. The stock price soars. No longer in danger of being sold, Tesla Motors, under the leadership of the extraordinary Elon Musk, pays off its loans and moves forward with the dream of replacing gasoline engine-driven vehicles with all-electric cars.

As Daniel Boone blazed a new trail through the wilderness to Kentucky, so Musk, a self-made billionaire, and often called the Tony Stark (from *Avengers* movie fame) of our time, also opened up new frontiers. Musk's world differs totally from Boone's, and the two individuals are as different as an ax is to an iPhone, but their leadership has many similarities. Like Boone, Musk inspires others to achieve more than they think they can achieve. Like pathfinders of the past, Musk has the heart of an explorer and an unstoppable drive to get the job done. Musk is a disruptor, a dreamer, an extraordinary leader, and an innovator. Innovation needs a mission, and Musk supplied a mission that has inspired teams of motivated innovators that are disrupting multiple industries that include all-electric cars, space, energy, and infrastructure. Like Boone, Musk is an example of a leader who consistently exceeds expectations.

Whether it is Boone or Musk, to accomplish anything, leaders must start, follow through, and finish. Getting started is hard. It is the most important step towards finishing. We all find excuses not to start, and when we do, we get very little done. Do not spend forever planning, researching, getting in the mood, or preparing—just start! We live in a world full of distractions. Reducing these distractions, turning off the plethora of screens that invade our time, is an act of focus. There is always another small task, email, or text message to consume your attention and blunt your focus. Getting started is crucial. Many people have good ideas, great intentions, and fanciful aspirations, but nothing happens until you act. For every journey, never underrate the importance of taking the first step. Deciding to act, and making the initial move forward, is the first step to winning. To learn, adapt, grow, and succeed, you must first get into the game. Start now and iterate later. Prepare, but do not wait for a perfect plan or circumstance. It does not require excellence to learn, but it is impossible to learn if you never start. Like Boone or Musk, everything after the first step is adapting to circumstance and taking advantage of opportunities. The *Tao Te Ching*, an ancient Chinese book of wisdom attributed to the Confucian scholar Lao Tzu around the 6th century BC, said that a journey of 1,000 *li* (a *li* is roughly equal to a third of a mile) begins with the first step. Lao Tzu was expressing the truth that great undertakings start from humble beginnings. People follow leaders like Boone and Musk for many reasons, but primarily because they know the answer to "Why."

Find Out Why

"The two most important days in your life are the day you are born and the day you find out why." Steve Harvey

Your first, critical step on your leadership journey is to take a moment to reflect and ask yourself this important question: "Why do I want to be a leader?" This is a fundamental question that every leader must tackle. The sooner you discover your Why, analyze it, know it, learn from it, and embrace it, the better you will know yourself. Knowing your Why takes serious thought, consideration and internal reflection. Contrary to countless citations on the Internet, Mark Twain (Samuel L. Clemens), author and humorist, never said: "The two most important days in your life are the day you are born and the day you find out why." I wish he had, as it seems like the sort of pithy and funny quip that Mark Twain might offer an attentive crowd. Instead, it took a 20th-century humorist and news reporter, Steve Harvey, in 2011, to bring this quote, and its plausible, but incorrect association, with Twain, into mass circulation. Whether the idea comes from Twain or Harvey, knowing your Why is a powerful life tool and a bit of wisdom that we must embrace as all knowledge starts with self-knowledge.

Bestselling author, motivational speaker, and explainer Simon Sinek has made a successful business out of teaching people to find their Why. Sinek cuts through the noise and delivers a powerful message about the value of knowing your Why and the reason you should start with Why. He believes that your Why is the purpose, the cause or belief, that inspires you to do what you do. Discovering your Why makes you go. It is your leadership fuel. If your Why is impelling enough, it can inspire others to follow you. Sinek believes that most people know what they do, some know how to do it, but very few know why they do it. "Before we can stand out," Sinek explains, "we must first get clear on what we stand for."

Why Should People Follow You?

People will not follow you until they know why they should follow you, and they will not buy into your leadership and follow you with enthusiasm and commitment until they learn why you are leading them.

Sinek described this combination of why, how and what as the Golden Circle: "Why" is in the center and relates to purpose; "How" is on the next ring and is the method to achieve the Why; "What" is on the outer ring and is the result of your Why, corresponding to an outcome, product or end state. Sinek teaches that most people start with What, then How, and finally Why, and that this order is inherently flawed. Sinek believes that effective leaders start with Why and work from the center of the Golden Circle outwards. Starting by asking the important question, "Why do I do what I do? What drives me to do this?" aims at the heart of your motivation to do anything, especially lead others. As Sink puts it, "People don't buy what you do. They buy why you do it." If leadership is influence—the leader influences people to follow—then for people to follow you with conviction, they must buy into your Why.

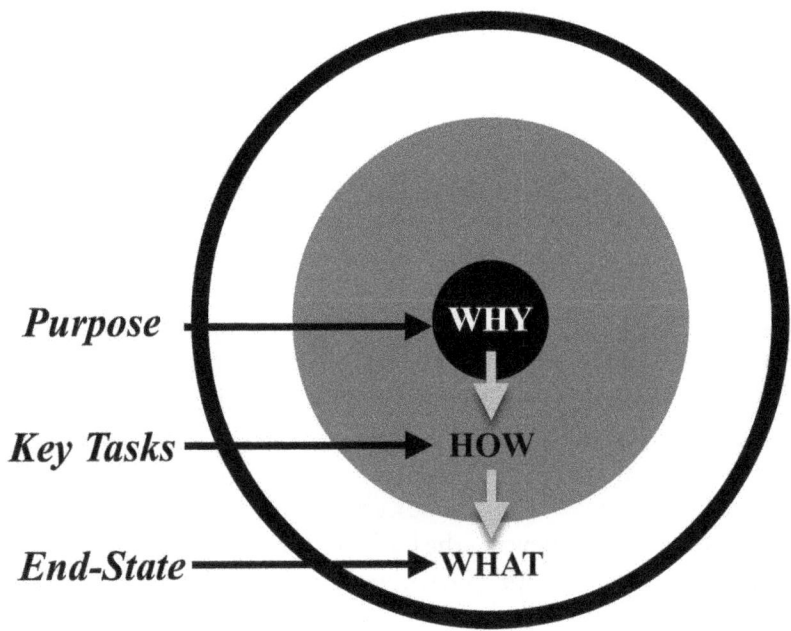

Simon Sinek's Golden Circle—Modified for Leader's Intent

Adding the words Purpose (reason), Key Tasks (process), and End-State (outcome) to Sinek's diagram helps to explain the meaning of the Golden Circle. Your Why relates to your purpose, the reason for what you are doing. How you do something, is a process that you can list as key tasks. What is your end-state or intended outcome. If you first understand your purpose, the key tasks, and end-state become easier to visualize and create. This "Golden Circle" illustration is derived from: Simon Sinek, *Start with Why* (New York Portfolio: Illustrated edition October 20, 2009) p.37.

People will not follow you until they know why they should follow you, and they will not follow you with enthusiasm and commitment until they learn why you are leading them. Sinek says: "If you hire people just because they can do a job, they'll work for your money. But if you hire people who believe what you believe, they'll work for you with blood and sweat and tears." Sinek also understands the difference between a leader and a manipulator: "There are only two ways to influence human behavior: you can manipulate it, or you can inspire it... The Why can help set a vision to inspire people. The Why can guide us to act with purpose, on purpose." Acting with purpose focuses energy to get the job done. Purpose drives you to continue when others quit. It helps you identify meaningful goals and prioritize between the important and unimportant. If others believe in your Why, your reason for action, it can motivate them to join you in that focus and you can lead them to accomplish goals they may not have thought possible.

Leaders who know why they are leading and act with purpose make the difference between getting to the destination or staying put; between action and inaction. Leaders move projects forward, ideas to realization, teams to grow, businesses to profit, and nations to succeed. Poor leaders can bring all these things to ruin. Manipulative leaders can cause confusion, waste, hardship, misery and pain. If you lead for the wrong purpose, then you are actually not a leader, but merely a manipulator. A manipulator is a person who controls or influences others in clever or unscrupulous ways. You will meet many manipulators along your lifelong leadership journey. It will be essential for you to know the distinction between a leader and a manipulator. Manipulators believe that leadership is merely a bag of tricks, filled with carrots and sticks, to entice or force people to do their bidding. Manipulators are cynics at heart. The dissimilarity between a manipulator and a leader goes to the soul of leadership.

John Maxwell, one of my mentors and a leadership author and expert, believes that understanding your Why comes down to three questions that people need to know: "Do you care for them? Will you help them? Can they trust you?" These three questions aim at the heart of your Why. If they understand your Why, and trust your purpose, people will follow you to the stars. Maxwell says that understanding your purpose is the key to success in leadership and in life. Successful people know their purpose in life. These people take the time to ponder, articulate, and write their purpose. The act of writing their purpose is a powerful act of focus. Their purpose is always a work in progress that they review and sharpen as they travel along their leadership journey, but it is useful as it acts like a guiding star to keep them on course.

In short, they understand their Why and this generates confidence. Knowing Why is powerful. It is the source of influence. If you know your Why, you can lead with confidence.

Know Yourself

"Knowing yourself is the beginning of all wisdom." Aristotle

What does it mean to know yourself? How does knowing yourself help you to learn, face challenges, and overcome hardships? If knowing yourself is central to successful leadership, then knowing your Why will help you know more about yourself. How do you discover your Why? Ask this question: What legacy do I want to leave? If you can answer this question, you are taking an important step to knowing yourself. Live the way you want to be remembered. If you do, then you are on the path to living a successful life. You will also have unlocked a key to knowing yourself. Socrates, the great ancient Greek philosopher, said the greatest dictum is to "know thyself." As Ronald Gross stated in his book, *Socrates' Way: Seven Keys to Using Your Mind* (Penguin, 2002), "Socrates didn't not [sic] contend that following him was 'the way'—just a way to find your way... As Socrates demonstrated, we only become ourselves most fully through our relationships with others: friends, mentors, and those we love and who love us." Aristotle, a pupil of the great Socrates, took this idea one step further and said: "Knowing yourself is the beginning of all wisdom."

Crucibles

You learn best who you truly are by successfully navigating a crucible. Everyone has challenges and hardships. It is often during these hard times that severely test you when you learn what you are made of. A crucible is an event or situation that is a severe trial and leads to the creation of something new. According to the Merriam-Webster dictionary, the word "crucible" appears related to the Roman Latin words for cross, but it derives from the Medieval Latin word *crucibulum*, which is the name for a special, heat-resistant clay pot used to melt metals. In the *crucibulum*, metals were fused with other liquefied metals. The result was a stronger, tougher and more resilient alloy. Each of us has a tensile strength, and we can make that resiliency stronger with discipline and practice. An enormous challenge can become a crucible that tests what you are made of. What makes you carry on when things get difficult and when others quit?

> ## Crucibles
>
> **You will experience tough times in your life. Everyone endures challenges and hardships. Turning a challenge into a learning experience is a key ability of an outstanding leader.**

The United States Army's Ranger School is an example of a crucible I experienced. Ranger School is the toughest school in the Army. Only a few earn the coveted Ranger Tab, the uniform insignia that distinguishes the wearer as a graduate of one of the most powerful leadership courses in the world. I will never forget the day I arrived at Fort Benning, Georgia to take on the challenge of Ranger School, a 61-day combat leadership course. I reported in on the second day of August and the temperature was hot enough to melt the paint off a steel helmet. Two hundred and sixteen Ranger Candidates stood with me as we entered Ranger School that morning. Sixty-one days later, less than half would graduate.

For the next two months, we slept very little, ate less, ran countless miles before dawn, endured unending hours at the mud-drenched obstacle course, affectionately known as the "worm pit," suffered innumerable sessions of harassment, instruction and inspection, executed dozens of chin-ups and pull-ups, struggled with hundreds of push-ups, all exacted by a cadre of hardcore, mean-spirited Ranger Instructors whose sole purpose in life appeared to be to convince us to quit. Every Ranger Candidate was a volunteer and could resign from the training at any time. To end the madness, a Ranger Candidate merely had to say, "I quit," and the pain and persecution would end. No more 15-mile cadence runs at 3 a.m. No more days with three hours of sleep. No more Ranger Instructor screaming at you while you stood at attention with sweat dripping off your face from the 100°F Georgia heat. Several candidates quit in the first week and we never saw them again. Others exited as the grinding physical and mental pressure took its toll. By the second week, we were down to around 170 Ranger Candidates.

To graduate, everyone had to complete the three weeks of Benning Phase, three weeks of Mountain Phase, and three weeks of the Florida Swamp Phase.

During this crucible, I learned that happiness in life had a lot to do with sleep—nothing more and nothing less. We ate only one meal a day, usually a combat "C" ration or a dehydrated long-range-patrol ration; everyone lost weight. When we talked to one another, the conversation inevitably turned to sleep and food. Some of my Ranger buddies began making lists of all the food they would eat after they graduated. The training continued without a break, and the Ranger cadre tested us as leaders at every step along the way. Each candidate had to successfully lead multiple patrols comprising groups of 12–50 Ranger Candidates. Each patrol was a leadership test and leading successful patrols was required to graduate. The cadre could grant you another chance to lead if you failed one patrol. Strike out a second or third time and you were cut from the course. At graduation in October, why were only 106 of the original 216 candidates present to become Rangers? The answer: each individual's character, competence, and commitment determined his fate. By the end of the course, we knew Who we were, Why we were in the Army, What was required to lead, and How we could overcome any hardship, no matter how severe. We knew our strengths and weaknesses and recognized that we had gained the confidence to adapt, improvise, and overcome any challenge. We realized that the instructors at Ranger School were some of the best leaders in our Army, and what we had endured was a lifelong gift. After this crucible, everything else seemed easy.

Lead Yourself First

**You cannot be a pathfinder without first leading yourself.
Know yourself, lead yourself, then lead others.**

A fundamental lesson I learned from Ranger School is that we all face crucibles in life. How we adapt, improvise, overcome, and endure is the measure of our leadership. During your leadership journey, you will face multiple challenges that will test you. If you embrace these experiences, you can grow and learn to overcome even greater challenges.

Discovering who you really are is harder than it sounds. As John Maxwell says: "To grow yourself you must know yourself." You will be stronger if you know your weaknesses, learn to avoid temptations, and know how to overcome challenges. If you know your strengths, you can reinforce these qualities to do the most good for yourself and those around you. Knowing how you will act and react in difficult situations will build confidence. You cannot be a pathfinder without first leading yourself. Know yourself, lead yourself, and then lead others.

> ## To Master Yourself, First Know Yourself
>
> Knowing yourself, your strengths and limitations are key attributes of an effective leader.
> Knowing both yourself and the competition are vital to victory.
> Knowing yourself means understanding your strengths and weaknesses.

Mastering Yourself

The Art of War is an ancient Chinese treatise on strategy and competition, attributed to Sun Tzu, the legendary Chinese general, writer and philosopher who lived in the 6th century BC. It has become a timeless guide on leadership for the military, government, top business schools and winning Chief Executive Officers (CEOs). The work represents a deep philosophy for winning any conflict, at multiple levels, and in all spheres of life. As Jessica Hagy, the author of the excellent recent study of Sun Tzu, *The Art of War Visualized*, said:

> In recent centuries, it's become not only the must-read book on military strategy (obviously), but it's also become the go-to guide for domination in business, politics, management, marketing, logistical planning, and even sports… *The Art of War* is massively popular because Sun Tzu's insights apply to all conflicts, great or small… It's less about war than it is about problem solving—it's a meta-metaphor. War is merely the stand-in noun for every hassle you've ever had in your life.

In *The Art of War*, Sun Tzu states: "So it is said that if you know your enemies and know yourself, you will not be put at risk even in a hundred battles. If you only know yourself, but not your opponent, you may win or may lose. If you know neither yourself nor your enemy, you will always endanger yourself." Knowing the adversary is key, as we learn everything from the competition. Knowing yourself means understanding your strengths and weaknesses. Knowing both yourself and the competition is indispensable to victory.

The Art of War emphasizes learning before leading, gaining knowledge of yourself, the opposition, and the circumstances, before deciding and acting.

Overcoming the competition and generating success for the team is the leader's end state. In the business world, the competition could be another company, or it might be a situation involving a difficult project with limited resources and a hard deadline. In war and competition, this involves a competitor with antithetical goals. Leaders who know themselves make better choices and their decision-making becomes the engine of their leadership. According to Sun Tzu, a winning leader learns to add the right people to the team to cover the leader's weaknesses and enhance the leader's strengths. This kind of thinking makes the team become greater than its individual parts as the team reinforces the leader's positive qualities and shores up the leader's flaws. Lao Tzu, the 6th-century Confucian scholar who wrote the *Tao Te Ching*, translated as *The Book of the Way and of Virtue*, said: "Mastering others is strength. Mastering yourself is the true power." If you know yourself, you know which way to go and you can set the path.

Mastery

"Knowing others is intelligence; knowing yourself is true wisdom. Mastering others is strength; mastering yourself is true power."
Lao Tzu

One reason that knowing yourself is so exasperating and difficult is our human tendency for self-deception. Avoiding self-deception requires separating ego from reality. This is no small task. Mark Twain believed that a leader must "know thyself" and wrote in his autobiography: "When a person cannot deceive himself the chances are against his being able to deceive other people." He continued: "We do not deal much in facts when we are contemplating ourselves." Knowing yourself helps you master other things as well. Theodore Roosevelt, the hero of the Spanish–American War and the 26th president of the United States, said: "Unless a man is master of his soul, all other kinds of mastery amount to little." Napoleon Hill, an influential leadership scholar and author of the 20th century, put it best: "If you do not conquer self, you will be conquered by self."

According to Benjamin Franklin, one of the greatest men of his age, a Founding Father of the United States, and a co-author of the Declaration of Independence, "There are three things extremely hard: steel, a diamond, and to know one's self." Franklin started a journey of self-awareness at a young age.

His life is an amazing story of self-improvement, discovery, lifelong learning, and leading and is worth studying. Franklin started off dirt-poor, the son of a soap- and candle-maker who had 17 children. Young Benjamin received only two years of formal education before he went to work as an apprentice at his brother's print shop. Franklin was a pathfinder, not a path-follower. Surrounded by books, he became a voracious reader and devoured every book he could find. He wanted to learn about everything, and he became a self-taught intellectual and polymath who never lost the common touch. He taught himself to be an expert writer and communicator. His yearly almanac, *Poor Richard's Almanack*, became one of the most vital, single points of knowledge in the Thirteen Colonies, selling nearly 10,000 copies per year from 1732 to 1758, in a time when books were printed by hand-powered printing presses.

Franklin worked to improve his body and mind, and he became a renowned athlete. In his time, most people could not swim. Franklin taught himself to swim by jumping into Philadelphia's Schuylkill River and swimming increasingly long distances. His swimming exploits became legendary, and were finally recognized in 1968, when he was posthumously created an honorary member of the International Swimming Hall of Fame. Franklin was still making news 178 years after his death! Besides swimming, Franklin was also a bodybuilder. He intuitively knew that his body and mind were part of the same system.

Franklin is a tremendous example of how "learning how to lead yourself" enables you to lead others. For the 18th century, he became a combination of today's John Grisham (best-selling author), Dave Ramsay (financial author and anti-debt evangelist), Bill Gates (inventor, technologist and philanthropist), Jeff Bezos (entrepreneur), Elon Musk (multi-industry disruptor), and Nelson Mandela (political leader) all in one. He was a self-taught and self-made man. He achieved this starting from very humble beginnings, fired by his own passion to learn, explore and lead. Among his many accomplishments, he was a leader in science (credited for discovering electricity); invention (he invented bifocals, the rocking chair, the Franklin stove, and much more); philanthropy (he endowed the Philadelphia Library); government (he established the first volunteer fire company, the first hospital, and as Joint Postmaster General, he made the post office in the Thirteen American Colonies effective and profitable for the first time in 1760); and was a central political leader in America's revolution and battle for independence from Great Britain. Franklin attributed his success to first knowing himself. He is quoted as saying: "Observe all men; thy self [sic] most."

Choose to be a Pathfinder

The more you know about your strengths and weaknesses, the more you will understand what leadership elements you need to improve and sharpen. If you truly know yourself, you can learn to lead others. Leaders are pathfinders. Pathfinders learn the path, walk the path, and guide others to the destination.

If you truly know yourself, you can learn to lead others and become a pathfinder by learning the path, walking the path, and guiding others to a destination. Knowing the path becomes an exercise of knowing the "self." As Lao Tzu said: "He who knows others is clever; he who knows himself has discernment." If you want to be an exceptional leader, work first on yourself.

One of the best ways to gain self-awareness is to ask the right questions. Keep them positive and you will usually find answers that are also affirmative. Franklin would start his day off with the question, "What good shall I do this day?" and ended his day with the question, "What good did I do today?" He was not interested in what he did well. He was interested in what good he did that day, for he felt that doing good made a lasting impact on other people, his community, his nation, and the world.

Work on Yourself

If you want to be an exceptional leader, work first on yourself.

Franklin invented many useful devices, including the lightning rod. He was fascinated by electricity and wanted to understand its powers. For the 18th century, Franklin was a "storm chaser" as he would ride a horse, wildly at full gallop in the darkness at night, into the area beneath a lightning storm. It seems remarkable to us, as we take our knowledge for granted, but people were unsure in the 18th century if lightning was a discharge of electricity or something else. Franklin desired to discover if lightning was electricity, and he developed many experiments to prove it. He transformed his home into a laboratory to investigate the phenomenon and the study of electricity became, for a time, his sole focus. During one experiment, he accidentally shocked himself with "a universal blow throughout my whole body from head to foot, which seemed within as well as without; after which the first thing I took notice of was a violent quick shaking of my body."

In June 1752, Franklin conducted the famous kite-with-a-metal-key experiment in a flashing lightning storm and held a kite-line while his 21-year-old son William stood nearby as his witness. In this dangerous experiment, Franklin saw the key on the string sparkle with electricity and realized lightning's true nature: it was electricity! Luckily, Franklin survived these experiments, and through these experiences, he learned ways to protect buildings from the hazards of lightning. After more experimentation, Franklin designed iron lightning points—lightning rods—that would "catch" the lightning, carry the charge along a metal wire, and safely draw it into the ground. In his diary, Franklin wrote:

> May not the knowledge of this power of points be of use to mankind, in preserving houses, churches, ships, etc., from the stroke of lightning, by directing us to fix, on the highest parts of those edifices, upright rods of iron made sharp as a needle... Would not these pointed rods probably draw the electrical fire silently out of a cloud before it came nigh enough to strike, and secure us from that most sudden and terrible mischief!

Creating the lightning rod was an amazing achievement, and Franklin could have sold the idea and become instantly wealthy. Instead, desiring to do the greatest good, he gave his invention away for free, and in this act, he not only guarded countless buildings from the ravages of a lightning strike and saved thousands of lives, he was subsequently regarded as both good and wise.

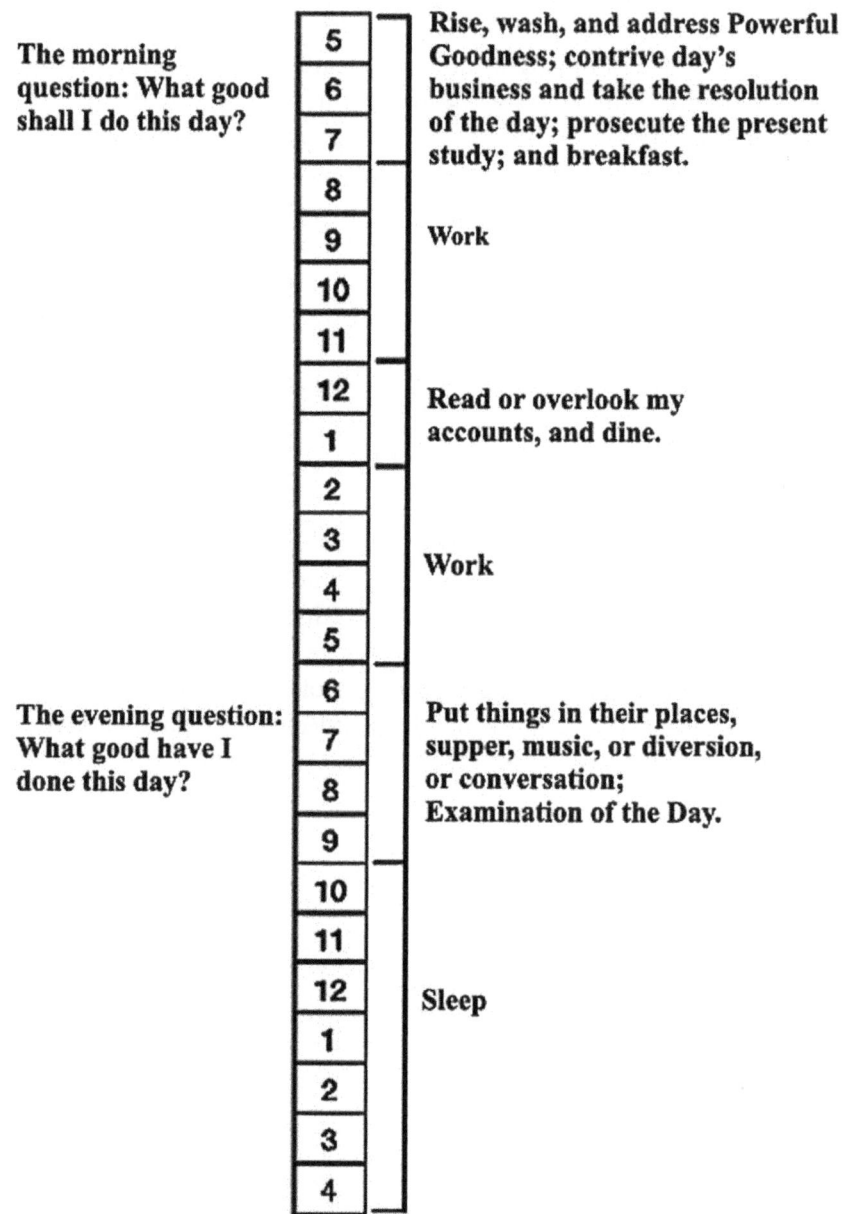

Benjamin Franklin's Daily Schedule

For Franklin, doing good meant doing something for someone else or for a cause greater than self. Franklin understood the power of knowing himself. He used daily reflection to further his self-knowledge. By examining his actions every evening with the question, "What good did I do today?," he taught himself to align his actions with his purpose and make the most of his available time to benefit himself and others. Through this method, Franklin could generate his creative abilities and leadership to do immense good. He crafted a daily list focused on doing something good every day. Although there is no evidence that Franklin studied the Chinese *Tao Te Ching*, he showed throughout his life that he understood: "Knowing others is intelligence, knowing yourself is true wisdom." The more you truly know yourself and continually seek self-improvement, the better you will lead others. The more you know of your strengths and weaknesses, the more you will know what to work on and what to guard against.

Daily Reflection

"What good did I do today?" Benjamin Franklin

Self-assessment

Self-assessments are hard. Imagine you are interviewing yourself for a critically important job. You are applying for a leadership position at LeadXYZ, a new start-up company with unlimited potential, but only a few dozen employees. LeadXYZ provides leadership coaching, training, and education for organizational leaders across the globe. LeadXYZ is ready to expand and has the funding to launch a new product. You are being interviewed for a job that will involve creating and leading a 25-person team of experts. Your team will form the cutting edge of the company, their "A Team." You will be required to hire and develop your team. The success of your organization and the livelihood of the company will depend on how well you lead.

In your mind's eye, review the leadership experiences you have had in the past and project them into this new situation at LeadXYZ. It does not matter if you have previous experience leading a small group, a large team, or members of your family. Place yourself into the scenario of leading the "A Team."

After reflecting on this situation and visualizing your own leadership in action, it is time to rate your leadership on the "Leadership Self-Assessment

Rating" form on page 19. This exercise is valuable for both emerging and experienced leaders. To make a proper self-assessment, think and reflect on the statements before selecting a number between 0 and 10, with 10 being the best rating. Tally the numbers at the end of the assessment and divide that number by 10. This is your leadership rating. Mark it on the subsequent page titled "Leadership Self-Assessment."

Leadership Self-Evaluation Rating

Rate yourself for each of the ten questions below, 1–10, with ten being the highest and best result. Then, add up the total of all ten questions and divide that number by ten. This is your leadership self-evaluation on a 1–10 scale.

1. When I am surprised, I brush off the shock as quickly as possible, assess the situation, and take action. 0 ⟷ 10

2. I lead by example and set the example. 0 ⟷ 10

3. I am a good follower. 0 ⟷ 10

4. I am trusted, and build trust within my team, with other teams, and with those that I follow. 0 ⟷ 10

5. I articulate a clear vision and intent to my teammates before we start a project or task. 0 ⟷ 10

6. I listen intently to those on my team. 0 ⟷ 10

7. I make timely and correct decisions. 0 ⟷ 10

8. I look for opportunities to praise teammates when they are doing a good job. 0 ⟷ 10

9. I take time, every day, to teach, coach, and mentor others to grow more leaders. 0 ⟷ 10

10. I take time at the end of the day to reflect on what I have done well and what I need to improve. 0 ⟷ 10

TOTAL = _____ ÷ 10 = SELF EVALUATION _____

Will LeadXYZ hire you? If your rating was less than a 10, do not feel bad. I have never met a perfect 10-level leader, but I have known some that came close. If I showed them this scale and told these "top" leaders that I rated them as a nine or 10, almost all of them would tell me I was paying them a greater compliment than they deserve, as they still had much to learn. This is one reason I rated them so high. Your rating is a snapshot of who you think you are right now. If you gave this same rating to those you lead, or those who know you well, how much would the rating differ? This can seem like an insignificant question, but it is central to understanding who you are. This difference is the variation between how we see ourselves and how others see us. If the variation is high, then reflect on whether what you say is actually what you do. The relationship between words and actions is the basis for trust.

Wisdom and Intelligence

"Knowing others is intelligence, knowing yourself is true wisdom."
Lao Tzu

By now, you have learned that leadership is a journey, and it represents a dynamic relationship between you and your team. Your leadership rating will move up and down this scale with every situation and different group you lead. If you know yourself and reflect upon your strengths and weaknesses as a leader, you can continually improve and learn to adapt quickly to new leadership situations. Contemplate this rating and discuss it with a trusted friend to gain another point of view. Keep this initial rating in mind as you continue your journey through this book.

After this self-assessment, the critical question to ask is: "Do you know yourself?" If you do, you have self-awareness and understand your strengths and weaknesses. Understanding your strengths and weaknesses allows you to compensate for shortcomings by having members of your team minimize your blind spots and inform you when they see risk. Knowing your strengths will give you the confidence to succeed. If you do not know your strengths and weaknesses, and delude yourself with false impressions of your abilities, your illusions may be shattered in the crucible of the real world. To avoid this, reflect, as you did in your self-assessment, and make periodic assessments. As you age, you will change, gaining knowledge and experience along the way. Combining these two offers the possibility of wisdom. There is no greater wisdom than knowing yourself. Life is short, and it becomes harder if you do not take time to reflect. Reflecting on your day and analyzing the impact of your daily leadership actions is a powerful tool that you can use to assess your own leadership journey.

Menander, the ancient Athenian playwright and dramatist, offers excellent advice on how to know yourself: "Know thyself means this, that you get acquainted with what you know, and what you can do." Notice the emphasis is on what you *can* do, not what you *cannot* do. As a leader, you will often hear your teammates lamenting on what they cannot do. This is an excuse. Leaders focus on what they can do and do not waste time thinking about "can't." Knowing what you know and what you can do provides a pattern that can render insight. Honing your perception of yourself is a valuable enabler. Your self-assessment is an initial evaluation of your leadership. After finishing this book, it will be useful for you to do this analysis a second time and see how you rate yourself. You should also use this self-assessment tool for other people to rate you and provide you their view of your leadership abilities. Your self-assessment may or may not match their rating. This is because we think more of ourselves than we do of others. As imperfect human beings, we often justify our negative actions that we would never let others get away with. Honestly assessing your leadership, therefore, is taxing, but it is impossible if you never try. Getting candid feedback from others is an excellent tool to help you build self-awareness.

Making self-assessment a habit, as Franklin did every evening, is a powerful way to learn who you are and how well you lead. Setting aside some time each day to reflect on your personal actions and growth as a leader can improve your self-image and confidence. If you want to create good leadership habits, carve out five minutes of uninterrupted time each day for reflection and self-assessment. The act of doing this and taking some time to think can be tremendously impelling. Turn away from all distractions and set a time to focus, think, and reflect. Thought is energy. You become what you think. With the power of thought, our minds can form and reorganize synaptic connections, especially in response to learning or experiences. This is called neuroplasticity, something many professional athletes know and practice. It is your means to develop higher levels of performance. A short period of daily reflection can change how you think and help you form new and positive habits. Create a quiet space, set aside undisturbed time, and let your mind totally focus on one goal, learning from each day and pledging to be a better leader and a better person than you were the day before. Ask yourself: What did I do today? What did I do well? What did I learn?

In every effort at self-improvement, time is the critical discriminator. Each day, we are all allotted the same amount of time. There is an enormous difference between being busy and doing something productive. If you want something badly enough, you can block off all distractions and interruptions and focus on mastering the desired skill or goal. Win the morning, for instance, and you have a better chance to win the day. Start each morning by tackling your most significant task first, and you will accomplish more. Be prepared each day to make the most of your time as a leader. If you want to be a world-class leader, take time to reflect and learn from your day's actions. Using that time wisely, with a focused, persistent, and undistracted approach, is fundamental to your growth as a leader. John Maxwell put it this way: "The unsuccessful person is burdened by learning and prefers to walk down familiar paths. Their distaste for learning stunts their growth and limits their influence." If learning is a burden for you, change your thinking. Learning is crucial to growth. Never stop learning.

Thought

Thought is energy. You become what you think.
With the power of thought, our minds can change form, and reorganize synaptic connections, especially in response to learning or experiences.

Marcus Aurelius, the Stoic philosopher and Emperor of Rome who led the Empire and its legions from 161 to 180 AD, took knowing himself seriously. History depicts Marcus as one of the last of the "Five Good Emperors" of Rome. He took time from his hectic schedule to study his own leadership and reflect on his actions every day. While at war, on campaign with his legions against the enemies of Rome, Marcus wrote his daily contemplations. He did not write these for publication, but rather to allow himself to analyze his daily efforts as leader and emperor. These writings represented his inner-most thoughts on self-improvement and how to become a more effective leader and a better man. Nearly thirteen hundred years after Marcus died, his 12 scrolls were published as *The Meditations*. Marcus argued that you can never truly know yourself with absolute certainty, but that you can know yourself well enough to be yourself. Marcus's *Meditations* highlight the power of reflection to improve your character, competencies, and commitment as a leader. Marcus believed that personality is the "developed self." He understood the power of the focused mind and its impact on leadership development. He said in his *Meditations*: "Such as are thy habitual thoughts, such also shall be thyself; for the soul is dyed by its thoughts." Marcus reasoned that an excellent leader develops and strives to "be thyself." Centuries later, William Shakespeare, the greatest playwright and author in the English language, would coin what Marcus Aurelius discussed with the phrase: "To thine own self be true."

Be Yourself

In *The Meditations*, Marcus Aurelius realized that you can never truly know yourself with absolute certainty, but that you can know yourself well enough to be yourself.

Knowing yourself is an important step to raising your leadership awareness. Warren Bennis, an American scholar, organizational consultant and leadership author, put it this way: "Becoming a leader is synonymous with becoming yourself. It is precisely that simple, and it is also that difficult." Self-awareness is a vital part of being a leader. e. e. cummings, the celebrated 20th-century American poet and essayist, once said: "It takes courage to grow up and become who you really are." Both Bennis and cummings learned the power of "knowing yourself" and used this awareness to positively influence others through their writing and teaching.

An article in the *Harvard Business Review*, "Getting It Done: New Roles for Senior Executives," by Thomas Hout and John C. Carter, concludes: "Senior executives were good at championing change but poor at changing themselves." This 1995 article addresses contemporary leadership challenges, proving the enduring nature of leadership conflicts. It is so relevant that it was republished in 2020. It seems reflection among senior leaders is atypical and this theme reinforces the satirical adage that there are only three types of leaders: Those who make things happen; those that watch things happen; and those who wonder what happened. Poor bosses fit all three categories of this axiom, and when they make things happen, they do so at the expense of the people on their team. It is easy for bosses to accomplish tasks at the expense of subordinates. Outstanding leaders attempt to create a win-win, whereby they focus on making things happen and elevating their team members. Leaders who see both sides of this coin, accomplishing the mission and taking care of their people, are exceptional. Understanding this contrast is a vital step in raising your leadership awareness.

The Manager and the Leader

Most of us have worked for a bad boss, as they are prevalent in every occupation. In business, a common corporate mentality is to drive rather than lead. Bosses compel their people to focus on the "bottom line," to "make the numbers." They will push people to accomplish these metrics at all costs, including wrecking teams and forcing employees out. "Hire and fire" is the mantra for too many businesses and organizations. The telltale sign of a declining organization is when you notice that everyone is too busy to think; there are too many meetings that seldom resolve problems, and no one brings up issues in order to avoid being assigned an additional assignment. Team leaders are working too hard on immediate tasks for them to develop their people to ensure long-term success. Bosses thrive in an environment where the focus is consistently on short-term tasks, versus long-term goals. Bosses, therefore, are common.

> **Are you a Boss, a Manager, or a Leader?**
>
> If you show me a successful team, I will show you an outstanding leader. If you show me a struggling team, I will show you a boss who needs to learn to lead. Managers synchronize resources. Leaders lead people. Which are you, a leader, a manager, or a boss?

You decide whether you are a boss or a leader. For our study of leadership, I define a boss as someone who dominates the group and manipulates their sense of purpose to achieve personal advancement. How do bosses succeed? This is a question that many inspirational studies of leadership avoid, but to comprehend this contradiction it is imperative to address both the positive and the negative aspects of leadership. To discern the disparity between a boss who accomplishes missions at the expense of the team, and a leader who both wins the mission and uplifts the team, let us examine the differences between a manager, a leader, and a boss.

Managers can and should lead, but not all managers are leaders. A manager coordinates the activities of resources in time, place, and purpose. Managers are vital to organizations as they make the process work and solve the myriad of tame problems (more about tame problems in Chapter 6, Shape your Destiny by Learning How to Decide) that occur every day. The primary resources that managers coordinate are people, time, and money. If they direct these resources to achieve a properly designated purpose, they usually keep the organization on track. If they do not, we consider them poor managers because they fail to synchronize the activities of people, time and money efficiently. Following the process often becomes a substitute for thinking. Leadership requires a higher order of thinking as leaders must solve problems that are not defined by process. A good manager, therefore, is not necessarily an excellent leader.

Managers

A manager coordinates the activities of resources in time, place and purpose. Managers are vital to organizations as they control the work process and flow and solve the myriad of tame problems that occur every day.

The difference between management and leadership lies in the purpose of their respective roles. Managers manage things. People dislike being managed when they sense they are being treated as a commodity. Most people prefer to be led rather than managed. They want to be treated as unique human beings and not lumped into the category of expendable resources. Managers who treat their people like commodities may be efficient at coordinating their actions in time, place and purpose, but seldom gain the effectiveness needed to create a high-performing team or organization.

Management of resources is important and good managers keep organizations operating. Every team needs efficient managers, but efficiency is not an end state. Efficiency is defined as the least waste of resources. Efficiency is measurable and repeatable, which is why it is so important to any organization. Efficiency means one plus one plus one equals three $(1 + 1 + 1 = 3)$. We can measure efficiency, quantitatively derived by the ratio of useful output to total input. Since the resources of time and money are the bottom line of many enterprises, managers closely monitor these. Most businesses spend significant time and energy to train their managers and create hierarchies to oversee the manager's efforts. Most organizations also create detailed regulations and precise procedures to guide the manager on how to act and what to decide in every imaginable situation. Managers are vital cogs in the machinery of process. Managers who stray from following the regulations are disciplined, reassigned, or fired. In short, managers execute the process, follow the instructions, and obey the rules. The measure of efficiency is to get the job done with the minimal expenditure of resources.

Efficiency of the individual parts does not guarantee a team's effectiveness. Effectiveness is the optimum use of resources and, with a team, the best use of the team's human capital to achieve more than just efficiency. Achieving effectiveness is about securing the highest results. Effectiveness means one plus one plus one is *greater* than three ($1 + 1 + 1 > 3$). When a team becomes more than just the sum of its parts, it demonstrates effectiveness. Elon Musk believes effectiveness is a mindset. According to Tim Urban, who interviewed Musk in 2015, Musk believes this mindset is analogous to the difference between a cook and a chef. A cook follows a recipe by the numbers, measuring each ingredient and applying it by the process laid out in the step-by-step instructions, and creates a tasty meal. Anyone who follows the recipe exactly can replicate the dish. We need and appreciate good cooks. A chef, on the other hand, accumulates basic ingredients and, with experience, inspiration and creativity, assembles a master dish that becomes a culinary experience. A chef experiments with each meal, develops a hypothesis of their culinary vision and iterates, adding a little of this, and a little of that, until the chef realizes the vision. Only a chef can create a culinary delight. The basic difference is that the cook focuses on being efficient while the chef focuses on being effective. One copies, the other creates. Both have value, but leaders who focus on being effective can transform their teams into high-performing organizations that are more than the sum of their individual parts.

People follow leaders and obey managers. Leaders also must manage resources, but they do not treat people as things, they lead them. Leaders are interested in both efficiency and effectiveness, with effectiveness trumping efficiency in most cases. Leaders view their followers not just as a vital resource, but as the essential and central element of any team or organization. Leaders do what it takes to communicate with their people and nurture their development as part of the team. Leadership is more important for any team, organization, or business than management, because management—the coordination of things in time, place, and purpose—is only part of the equation. Managers can be leaders, but leadership requires the manager to grow beyond the world of resources and process and into the world of people and interactions.

> ## Leaders
>
> Leaders treat people not just as a vital resource, but as the essential and central element of any team or organization ... Leadership is more important for any team, organization, or business, than management, because management—the coordination of things in time, place, and purpose—is only part of the equation.

Developing leaders, therefore, is much more difficult than creating managers. The conundrum is that leadership is simultaneously the least expensive and the most expensive resource of any organization. When you have effective leaders, your organization can achieve beyond expectations. When you have poor leaders—bosses—your organization will usually do the minimum required to make the boss happy. Leadership, therefore, seems to cost nothing when it works, but when there is no leadership, the cost is expensive indeed. Leaders who share the vision of the organization, who can communicate that vision, and who can motivate people to achieve that vision, are priceless. Developing these leaders requires a significant investment in people, and when an organization makes this choice, the results can be tremendous.

Many people incorrectly define all managers as leaders. When language is inexact, thinking is fuzzy. Managers who merely follow the process, procedures and regulations have little room for individual judgment. Managers who take initiative are leaders and should be recognized as such. Leaders who understand the process, procedures and regulations, but who are also empowered to lead their people beyond these restrictions and act in alignment with the organization's overall intent, can speed up the decision-making process and seize successes that would be impossible for mere managers.

Poor leaders, who internalize their role as the art of manipulation and coercion, are bosses. Bosses have no followers, only pawns. People who are treated as pawns seldom adopt the commitment required to win, they merely do what they need to do to get by. Leadership coach Ken Blanchard, a co-author of the mega-selling book *The One-Minute Manager* (HarperCollins, 1981), stated: "In the past a leader was a boss. Today's leaders must be partners with their people ... they no longer can lead solely based on positional power." He said partners, not buddies, and he is correct. Few people want a boss, but they are searching for a leader, committed to them, the team, and their long-term success. Bosses can get things done, especially in the short run, because they expend their people and resources to meet short-term goals. In business, there is a truism: "Employees don't quit their jobs, they quit their boss." As author Simon Sinek says, "A boss has the title. A leader has the people."

Knowing yourself is the first step in learning how to be a leader rather than a boss. "At the center of your being you have the answer to this; you know who you are and you know what you want," wrote M. J. Ryan, a bestselling author and executive coach to senior executives and entrepreneurs around the world. If you want to be a pathfinder, move beyond being a manager, avoid being a boss, and learn to lead. Try. Without trying, there is no growth and no accomplishment, no stretching of mind and heart. Leaders move forward and influence their teammates in ways that make them want to follow and grow. Pathfinders gain strength in tough times by knowing who they are and having confidence in what they can do. As John Maxwell puts it: "If you wouldn't follow yourself, why should anyone else?"

Are you a path-follower or a pathfinder? Most people are path-followers; they look for a route to follow and prefer one that is lined with signposts that show the way to the destination. They want someone to go before them and show them the way. "Leaders," Simon Sinek says, "are the ones who have the courage to go first and open a path for others to follow." It can take enormous courage to blaze a dangerous, fresh path—imagine the courage of Daniel Boone as his team hacked out the Wilderness Trail. There were no rest stops, restaurants, or comfortable hotels along the way. Danger lurked around every turn and the path forward was not assured. Anyone can guess which way to go, but it takes a leader, like Daniel, to get the group to the right destination and set rally points along the way that others can follow. In cases like this, the group seeks a leader, someone who will be their pathfinder; someone who learns the path, shows the path, and walks the path. The mark of leadership is the contrast between being a path-follower and a pathfinder.

As John Maxwell says: "Leaders know the way and show the way." Knowing your Why and understanding your purpose provides you with a strong conviction of direction that can steady you in the fiercest storm. The day you find your Why, therefore, is your first step in understanding yourself and becoming a leader. The next step is to follow the wisdom of Socrates by defining what you wish to understand. In the next chapter, you will investigate your understanding of Purpose.

Chapter Summary

1. In life, you can be a path-follower or a pathfinder. Be a pathfinder. You will rise to the level of your leadership. To accomplish anything, leaders must start, follow through and then finish.

2. Knowing yourself is an important step in raising your leadership awareness. If you know your strengths and weaknesses, you can act accordingly. One of the best ways to gain self-awareness is to ask the right questions.

3. It is during hard times, when you experience a crucible in your life and are severely tested by people and circumstances, that you learn who you really are. Embrace these experiences and learn from them. Always seek to be yourself and not try to act like someone else.

4. Thought is energy. Control your thoughts and you control your destiny. You become what you think. With the power of thought, our minds can change form, and reorganize synaptic connections, especially in response to learning or experiences.

5. A manager coordinates the activities of resources in time, place and purpose. Managers are vital to organizations as they make the process work and solve the myriad of tame problems that occur every day.

6. Leaders treat people, not just as a vital resource, but as the essential and central element of any team or organization. Leadership is more important for any team, organization, or business than management, because management—the coordination of things in time, place, and purpose—is only part of the equation.

7. Developing leaders is much more difficult than creating managers. When you have effective leaders, your organization can achieve beyond expectations. When you have poor leaders—bosses—your organization will usually do the minimum required to make the boss happy. Leadership, therefore, seems to cost nothing when it works, but when there is no leadership, the cost is high indeed.

Self-Assessment

Purpose

Find your "Why"

Know

Master Self

Duty

Path Follower

LEADERSHIP

Pathfinder

Reflect Process

Values

Outcome

Be Yourself

Crucibles

Goals

Thought

CHAPTER 2

Determine Your Purpose

The Path of Leadership Requires a Clear Sense of Purpose

He was only 16; he loved drawing and art and desired to make a difference in the world. He felt that he had some noble purpose that had been driving him all his young life. Then, events overseas pulled his attention. A great war had erupted in Europe and America was in the fight. He felt compelled to do his share and join the United States Navy to serve his country. He dropped out of school and went to the Navy recruiters. Rejected at the enlistment office for being under the legal enlistment age of 17, he volunteered for the Red Cross, became an ambulance driver, and was sent "over there." He arrived in France just after the armistice was signed but still served for a year, driving supply trucks and ambulances for an evacuation hospital in Paris. During this time with the Ambulance Corps, his sense of purpose was his driving force. Immersed in helping the wounded and lifting spirits, he tried to do everything he could to bring respite, and he expressed this in his drawings and cartoons. He drew humorous animals and images on the inside and outside of the canvas sides of his ambulance. When he was not driving, he was constantly drawing cartoons. Soon whimsical images covered his ambulance. Some of his work was so well appreciated that his artwork appeared in *Life Magazine* and the Red Cross newspaper. He believed his purpose was to raise people's spirits and encourage them to dream. He understood that his "Why" was to help people see outside of their troubles and seek the beauty of life. He believed: "All our dreams can come true, if we have the courage to pursue them." That young man was Walt Disney, who served during World War I, and later created Mickey Mouse, Donald Duck, Goofy, and many other unforgettable characters and stories. Leader, visionary and patriot, he also became the founder and CEO of one of the greatest entertainment companies in the world.

Finding your Why invokes knowing your purpose. The two are not synonymous but are closely related. Your Why is your reason for being. You begin by asking the questions to determine your core values, what you are passionate about, and what gives you meaning. Your Why does not have to be some grand, daunting effort for fame or glory, or about saving the world. In fact, it works best when we start with ourselves. It can be simply the act of not trying to be better than anyone else, to striving to be a better version of yourself every day. You have the choice to be your best self, to learn, grow, and act as you would like to be remembered. Take this Why and then create your purpose.

> ### Alignment with Purpose
>
> A clear purpose visualizes the destination and defines success. When you align your personal values, spirit and goals, you have focus. With focus, you can achieve a defined purpose and move people to action.

Your purpose statement impels you to act and provides a direction. Purpose is the ability to harness your determination to achieve your vision. You can motivate people to work together to accomplish a goal, but that effort only matters if you know where you are going. Movement without destination is merely walking around. For example, Elon Musk's purpose is to make humanity a two-planet species by developing the means to colonize Mars. He is fiercely focused on this goal, and with SpaceX, is taking significant steps to make this a reality. In Musk's case, purpose is everything. Purpose is powerful and a leader's value to the team is only as deep as the leader's purpose. Leading with purpose means the leader owns the goals and objectives and translates the parameters of success to the team. A clear sense of purpose is indispensable to successful leadership. It will not only help you become a more effective leader; it may also lead you to find happiness.

Purpose is about expanding beyond yourself. A clear sense of purpose can be a galvanizing and motivating force. German philosopher Friedrich Nietzsche once said, "He who has a why can endure any how." A more recent philosopher, Yogi Berra, also had a lot to say about purpose. Yogi was an American professional baseball catcher, team manager, and coach famous for his malapropisms and pithy, paradoxical statements. You may have heard the sayings "It ain't over till it's over" and "When you come to a fork in the road, take it." These Yogi-isms seem both paradoxical and funny, but there is wisdom within them, as they cause you to stop and think. The humor of these quips was electric, and reporters would do their best to be the first to print or broadcast a new Yogi-ism. Regarding knowing your purpose, Yogi Berra hit a home run: "You've got to be very careful if you don't know where you are going because you might not get there." While certainly humorous, it is patently true. Many people do not have a course in life. Visualizing the destination and setting a course is how a pathfinder finds the way. Knowing your purpose, therefore, is vital if you want to get to where you intend to go.

The Quality of Your Thoughts

"The happiness of your life depends upon the quality of your thoughts." Marcus Aurelius

What is your purpose as a leader? More deeply, what is your purpose in life? Aristotle used the concept of *telos* to describe a person's purpose. *Telos* is derived from the ancient Greek (τέλος for "end, purpose, or goal") to describe the aim and intention of any individual, and the moral concepts that guide them. If you lie, cheat and steal, your leadership will reflect this, and you will attract primarily liars, cheaters and thieves to your side. If you believe in honesty, fairness, and earning what you have worked for, then the people drawn to your leadership will normally be of a more positive character. Aristotle focused his attention concerning *telos* on a person's life goal. He believed that each of us has a life purpose and that our vital task in life is to understand, know and attain that purpose. Aristotle explained the purpose of life is earthly happiness that can be achieved only through reason and the development of virtue.

Marcus Aurelius took this thinking a step further by stating that the purpose of life was duty. He believed that every person and everything had a duty to perform. "Everything, a horse, a vine, is created for some duty," Marcus wrote in his *Meditations*: "For what task, then, were you yourself created? A man's true delight is to do the things he was made for." He believed that you have control of your mind, and therefore, you choose to either be in control or out of control, to work to achieve your purpose, or to squander the great gift of existence bestowed upon you when you were born. Marcus firmly believed that "The happiness of your life depends upon the quality of your thoughts." If those thoughts were directed at accomplishing your duty, Marcus would argue that you lived a noble life.

Living with a Purpose

"The purpose of life is not to be happy at all. It is to be useful, to be honorable. It is to be compassionate. It is to matter, to have it make some difference that you lived."
Leo Rosten

In the 1960s, Leo C. Rosten wrote about the meaning of happiness in a quote that has often been mis-attributed to Ralph Waldo Emerson, the 19th-century American author, poet and philosopher. Rosten said:

> The purpose of life is not to be happy—but to matter, to be productive, to be useful, to have it make some difference that you lived at all. Happiness, in the ancient, noble sense, means self-fulfillment—and is given to those who use to the fullest whatever talents God or luck or fate bestowed upon them. Happiness, to me, lies in stretching, to the farthest boundaries of which we are capable, the resources of the mind and heart.

Rosten, like Marcus Aurelius, understood that the purpose of life was not to be found in hedonistic pleasure, indulgence and saturation in entertainment. He would have viewed such a life as a waste and very selfish. There is a higher happiness to serving a purpose greater than yourself. Rosten discussed this idea in an article he published in *The Journal of General Education* (Volume 17, Number 3, October 1965, pp. 169–78) titled "The Myths by Which We Live." In this article, he restated the purpose of life as he saw it:

> Finally there is the myth which gives me the greatest pain: the myth that the purpose of life is happiness, and that you ought to have fun, and that your children ought to have fun. Where was it written that life is so cheap? Where was it written that life is, or should be, or can ever be free of conflict and effort and deprivation and sacrifice? ... the purpose of life is not to be happy at all. It is to be useful, to be honorable. It is to be compassionate. It is to matter, to have it make some difference that you lived.

For Rosten, if you know your purpose, and take steps every day to achieve that goal, you can find happiness.

To test this idea, think about your own life. Do you know your Why and your purpose? If so, do your work and daily activities move you toward your goal, even if you are only taking small steps each day along the path to achieving your *telos* (your aim and intention and the moral concepts that guide them)? As a case in point, imagine that you have not found your Why and are not living your purpose. Are you simply working for a paycheck? Imagine that you are working in a job that you hate, a job that is not fulfilling your Why or purpose but you are earning a salary to get by. You say to yourself that you will move onto a new job, but that day is always pushed into the future. You feel trapped. Why is working only for a paycheck so unfulfilling? Fulfillment makes a difference in your motivation to get the job done. Imagine, instead, that you are on a different path, that you know your Why, understand your purpose, and are working in a career where you are fulfilling both. Which path do you want to be on? If you don't know your Why and Purpose, how will you know the path?

So how can you really understand your purpose? Let us conduct a short thought experiment that was inspired from my study of Michael J. Gelb's book *How to Think Like Leonardo da Vinci*. In this exercise, you will draw a simple mind map to help illustrate a way to uncover your purpose. To begin, you will need a half-dozen differently colored pens or pencils. Over the next few pages you are going to complete various tasks, then you will bring all the results together on page 52, "My Mind Map."

Step 1: Create your own logo. Your logo is a visual representation of who you are. In ancient days, this might be your personal crest. Like a crest, it should be an emblem you are proud of, that represents you, your values, your goals and your highest aspirations. A personal logo becomes your brand, a symbol of your Who you are, and it should reflect your Why. Take some time to think about it and create a symbol of "who you are" that is meaningful. Do not worry about any lack of artistic talent; you can improve the logo later.

Creating a personal logo is a constructive exercise in self-awareness. Your logo does not have to be a work of art, neither should it be like the example provided, but it should come from your heart and your head, essentially a combination of feeling and thought. The example logo is provided to give you some ideas. It might be as explained as follows: Life and leadership is a journey and you are a pathfinder, represented by the person hiking on the left. The symbols from the top, left to right, may signify: Compass (Leadership); Hourglass (Making every moment count); Book (Lifelong Learning); Star (Duty and Purpose); and in the center, a Heart (Love). Your logo should be whatever inspires you to say: "This is me." It can be one image or several, but should be symbolic, not words. Our minds think in pictures. Be as visual as you can be.

Values

Values help define your individual leadership as they express your unique character. When you live by your personal core values consistently, and these values are congruent with your actions, you move closer to fulfillment.

Step 2: List your values. What values do you live by? Values help define your individual leadership as they express your unique character. When your values are congruent with your actions, you move closer to fulfillment. There are three broad categories of values: personal, moral and aesthetic. Personal values are values you endorse for yourself. Moral values are about right and wrong. Aesthetic values are used to categorize nature, taste and beauty. Your core values are a mixture of all three and represent your fundamental beliefs as a person. Stated another way, your core values define what you stand for, what you would fight for, and what you would sacrifice everything for. Knowing your core values helps you define who you are. Review the words in the catalog titled "A List of Values" and circle those you believe represent your personal values.

Abundance	Daring	Integrity	Relationships
Acceptance	Decisiveness	Intuition	Resilience
Accountability	Dedication	Joy	Resourcefulness
Achievement	Dependability	God	Responsibility
Advancement	Determined	Kindness	Responsiveness
Adventure	Diligence	Knowledge	Risk Taking
Advocacy	Duty	Leadership	Safety
Ambition	Empathy	Learning	Security
Appreciation	Encouraging	Love	Self-Awareness
Attractiveness	Energy	Loyalty	Self-Control
Autonomy	Enthusiasm	Making a Difference	Selflessness
Balance	Ethical	Meritocracy	Self-Reliance
Being the Best	Excellence	Mindfulness	Sensitivity
Benevolence	Expressiveness	Modesty	Service
Boldness	Fairness	Morality	Simplicity
Brave	Family	Motivation	Spirituality
Brilliance	Friendships	Nurturing	Stability
Calmness	Flexibility	Optimistic	Success
Caring	Focused	Open-Minded	Teamwork
Challenge	Freedom	Originality	Thankfulness
Charity	Fun	Passion	Thoughtfulness
Cheerfulness	Generosity	Patriotism	Traditionalism
Clear	Grace	Peace	Thrifty
Cleverness	Growth	Perfection	Trustworthiness
Community	Flexibility	Performance	Understanding
Commitment	Fun	Playfulness	Uniqueness
Compassion	Happiness	Popularity	Usefulness
Cooperation	Health	Power	Valor
Collaboration	Honesty	Personal	Versatility
Consistency	Humility	Development	Victorious
Contribution	Humor	Preparedness	Vision
Country	Inclusiveness	Proactive	Warmth
Courage	Independence	Professionalism	Wealth
Courtesy	Individuality	Punctuality	Well-Being
Creativity	Innovation	Quality	Wisdom
Credibility	Inspiration	Recognition	Zeal
Curiosity	Intelligence	Reflection	Zest for Life
		Reliability	

A List of Values

Listing your values is difficult. As hard as it may appear, this is worth your effort and an excellent way to strengthen your understanding of who you really are. It is okay to be aspirational and pick values you *want* to have, but a clear understanding of "who you are" is better served by recognizing and listing the values you live by. Ponder the values you circled and then pick the top seven that you wish to represent yourself. Selecting your top seven requires self-reflection and introspection. After choosing them, take a moment to prioritize the ones that are the most meaningful to you. For example, your top seven core values might include, in priority order: Courage, Leadership, Honesty, Diligence, Freedom, Resilience, and Learning. Another example may be: Faith, Family, Happiness, Humility, Inclusiveness, Nurturing, and Relationships. What is more important than the list, is your ability to articulate why these are your values, how you live by them, and why they are in the priority you listed. List your seven values, in priority, on the next page.

List Your Top Seven Values:

1. _____

   _____

   _____

2. _____

   _____

   _____

3. _____

   _____

   _____

4. _____

   _____

   _____

5. _____

   _____

   _____

6. _____

   _____

   _____

7. _____

   _____

   _____

Step 3: List your life goals. Life goals are long-range goals. Accomplishing worthy goals is the means to success. Goals are your aiming points to provide direction, but they only become reality if you act to develop the habits to achieve those goals. One way to understand your goals is to identify your habits. Habits are powerful. If your habits support achieving your goals, you will be more likely to succeed. Habits put good or bad practices on autopilot. Developing good habits is a worthy goal. If you are a habitual smoker, but your goal is to stop smoking, you will fail until you change your habits. If you want to be financially independent, review your budgetary and investment habit practices. If you have successful monetary practices, you can predict how long it will take to meet your financial goals. If you do not, then the goal is merely a wish, and wishes without action often remain unfulfilled. Look at your current habits and investigate if your actions support achieving your goals. If they do not, develop positive habits. If you want to be a lifelong learner, then the discipline of reading a new book every month supports that goal. For instance, the positive habit you need to develop to secure this goal is: "I will read a book every month as I am a lifelong learner." A great resource to understand the power of habits is James Clear's bestselling book, *Atomic Habits: An Easy & Proven Way to Build Good Habits & Break Bad Ones* (Avery, 2018). In this book, Clear "reveals practical strategies that will teach you exactly how to form good habits, break bad ones, and master the tiny behaviors that lead to remarkable results." Clear's theme is that tiny changes, reinforced over time, lead to big results. So, for example, if you want to start reading more, just read one page a day. Eventually, this turns into a habit of reading and becomes a discipline that can improve your life.

Writing down your life goals is a useful exercise. If you have never made a list of life goals, now is a good time to start. When you articulate your life goals, you set a clear path toward your desired destination. "If one does not know to which port one is sailing," quipped the Roman philosopher, statesman and dramatist Lucius Annaeus Seneca, "no wind is favorable." Setting a destination is the best way to catch the opportunities (Seneca's allusion to the wind) that arise in life. "Setting goals," says author and motivational speaker Tony Robbins, "is the first step in turning the invisible into the visible." Robbins set four secrets to effective goal setting: "1. Remember that the pursuit matters just as much as the goal. 2. Set a goal with the right scope in mind. 3. Focus on what you want, not what you don't want. 4. Don't stop after you've achieved your goal. 5. Don't worry about not achieving your goals." In addition to this advice, ponder where you want to be in 10 years and what goals are needed to get you there. Consider categories for these goals, such as family, career, education, spiritual, financial, and health. Take a "full-person" approach. For instance, listing only financial goals, and ignoring family and self-development goals, may define you as a one-dimensional person. Take 10–15 minutes to think about what is most important to you and then start writing. Once you have listed your goals, place the goal that best addresses your purpose and values first, followed by the other three. List your four goals on the next page.

My Life Goals

1. _____

_____

_____

2. _____

_____

_____

3. _____

_____

_____

4. _____

_____

_____

Contemplate these goals and then check them against the acid test of your current habits. Consider if your goals are in congruence with your purpose and values by asking: "Do my life goals help me achieve my purpose and express my values?"

Step 4: Know your Strengths. The next step is to list four personal strengths. These are your competencies. Competencies can be cognitive skills, the ability to process thoughts, and knowledge-based skills, the learning required to perform procedures and tasks. For instance, cognitive skills might include organizing, planning, moderating, or negotiating. These skills often involve the superior ability to maintain attention, focus, process information, recognize patterns, or remember information. Knowledge-based skills may be job-related, such as accounting, carpentry, computer science, design, engineering, legal or sales. If you listed computer skills as a strength, then you should know how to use the latest software and continually maintain proficiency. If problem solving is a strength, then you should be able to recall several difficult challenges that you solved in the recent past. As we used habits to be the acid test for goals, what you are good at should also be reflected in your positive habits. If you can identify your strongest positive habits, these should relate to your strengths. As habits provide insight to help you determine if a goal is real, or merely a wish, habits are also the building blocks of your personal strengths. Think about this carefully and then list your top four strengths.

My Top Strengths

1. _____

   _____

2. _____

   _____

3. _____

   _____

4. _____

   _____

Step 5: Write your Legacy. Your legacy is a simple statement of what you wish to be remembered for. Take time to think about how you make a difference, count your blessings, and consider what you already know is memorable in your life, then articulate your legacy. Your legacy statement is how you would like to live and be remembered. It should be a statement of your highest affirmations. Thinking about your legacy has nothing to do with your current age. Tomorrow is a gift yet to be received. What is your most lasting gift to others? You can think of your legacy statement as a gift for the people who you care about and who care about you. Your most important legacy is not the things you leave behind, for all things are transitory, but the memories of your actions that linger in other minds. Think deeply about this, and do not feel constrained when initially writing it. When complete, reduce your thoughts down to two or three brief sentences.

My Legacy

1. _____
   _____
   _____

2. _____
   _____
   _____

3. _____
   _____
   _____

Step 6: Document your life's purpose. Finally, using your logo, values, goals, strengths, and legacy as references, craft your statement of purpose. This is often the most challenging task in completing a personal mind map. Writing a succinct statement that describes the purpose of your life is a critical step in knowing yourself. Do you think there is a purpose to everything you do, or at least what you should do? Now is your chance to find out. Think about your logo, values, goals, strengths and legacy as building blocks to your purpose statement. Not knowing your purpose can lead you to unfortunate consequences. Rich Karlgaard, an American journalist, bestselling author, award-winning entrepreneur and speaker, explained knowing your purpose this way: "Purpose is a soft virtue—but it's what gives you steel in your spine."

Steel in Your Spine

"Purpose is a soft virtue—but it's what gives you steel in your spine."
Rich Karlgaard

Purpose is drive with direction. It helps move you forward and points you to a destination. It gives you the motivation to overcome adversity. If you develop a clear purpose, then you know where you want to go and every day you can take steps to move closer to your goal. Every step forward towards your purpose, no matter how small, is a victory. Purpose gives you something to live for greater than yourself. Looking outside yourself will help you to grow in multiple dimensions. Clarity of purpose generates greater impact. It allows you to communicate more convincingly. Once you have a purpose that fits who you are, you not only have a powerful tool for navigating career decisions and living successfully, but you will also increase your chances for happiness.

To determine your purpose, start by asking the right questions. What makes you happy? What provides you with the most challenging and engaging experiences? What are you passionate about, so passionate that you focus solely on it and lose track of time? What inspires you and gives you pride in accomplishment? Look at your seven values and think how they relate to your purpose. What is the one major action in life that you want to accomplish? What advice would your future self give you at this moment? Think about answers to these questions and write a brief sentence or two that defines your purpose in life. Do not overthink this; do it as quickly as you can and revise it later. Bravely attack this task; see what you develop and do not worry about being perfect. Just do it! Your purpose will evolve as you continually reflect upon it.

Your purpose is your mission statement. You developed it for yourself. Do not worry or care what anyone else will think about it. Use active voice: "My purpose is to…" Have the courage of conviction and write down in bold words your mission statement. Often, your first thought is true and on target. Focus your thoughts and decide. Writing your purpose statement clarifies what you want to accomplish and live for, and defines the person you are or want to be. Once you have completed your purpose, write it down in the area titled: "My Purpose Statement."

My Purpose Statement

My purpose is to _____

_____

_____

_____

_____

_____

_____

_____

_____

_____

_____

_____

_____

_____

_____

_____

_____

_____

Step 7: Create Your Personal Mind Map. Transfer the information you created in Steps 1–6 onto the blank form titled "My Mind Map." Your personal mind map is a snapshot in time that provides you with a picture of who you are, who you want to be, and where you want to go.

My Purpose:

My Values:

My Personal Logo

My Strengths:

My Goals:

My Legacy:

My Mind Map

Tony Buzan, an expert on the brain and learning, author of over 100 books, and the inventor of mind mapping, defined a mind map as: "[A] thinking tool that reflects externally what goes on inside your head. The mind map is like a Swiss Army knife for the brain. Anything I want to do in terms of thinking, contemplation, cognition, or remembering, creating, the mind map is the ideal tool for that… The brain thinks by imagination and association." Associating your purpose, values, strengths, goals, and legacy, you have created a unique visualization of who you are. To improve your understanding of mind mapping, check out Buzan's book *Mind Map Mastery: The Complete Guide to Learning and Using the Most Powerful Thinking Tool in the Universe* (Watkins Publisher, 2018). Creating your personal mind map is a remarkable effort of self-reflection and a valuable tool to help you become a better leader.

In this exercise, you have visualized your life. In one page, you have summarized who you are, who you want to be, and where you want to go. The more accurate your visualization, the more this page represents your true thoughts of who you are. Your rudimentary mind map is a snapshot in time that will help you sharpen your self-awareness and will take you one step closer to knowing yourself. Now that you have a better understanding or who you are, it is time to visualize a model of leadership and learn how to use this self-knowledge to become a better leader.

Chapter Summary

1. The path of leadership requires a clear sense of purpose.

2. Your purpose is a statement that puts your Why into action. Purpose is the ability to harness your determination to achieve your vision.

3. Understanding and finding your purpose is powerful. When you align your personal values, spirit and goals, you can focus your leadership. When your leadership is guided by a defined purpose, you can move people to action.

4. Why is working only for a paycheck so unfulfilling? Fulfillment makes a difference in your motivation to get the job done. Imagine, instead, that you are on a different path, that you know your Why, understand your purpose, and are working in a career where you are fulfilling both. Which path do you want to be on? If you do not know your Why and purpose, how will you know the path?

5. Visualization is a powerful tool. One way to visualize your purpose is to create a personal mind map. This mind map consists of:
   a. Creating your own personal logo helps you to "see" your purpose in your mind's eye.
   b. Listing your values. Values help define your individual leadership as they express your unique character. When you live by your personal core values consistently, and these values are congruent with your actions, you move closer to fulfillment.
   c. Listing your life goals. One way to understand your goals is to identify your habits. What you habitually do, you become. Aligning habits with goals is a means to achieve those goals.
   d. Listing your strengths. What are you good at?
   e. Writing your legacy. What do you wish to be remembered for?

6. Purpose gives you something to live for greater than yourself. Looking outside yourself will help you to grow in multiple dimensions. Clarity of purpose generates greater impact. It allows you to communicate more convincingly.

7. Your personal mind map is a snapshot in time that provides you with a picture of who you are, who you want to be, and where you want to go. This can be a remarkable effort of self-reflection and a valuable tool to help you become a better leader.

NOTES

Competencies
Self-Assessment
BE
Duty
Master Self
Purpose
Know
Character
Find your "Why"
Path Follower
Commitment
LEADERSHIP
Pathfinder
Values
Be Yourself
Crucibles
DO
Reflect
Process
Focus
Goals
KNOW
Visualize
Outcome
Thought

CHAPTER 3

Visualize Your Leadership Compass

What You Can Conceive and Believe, You Can Achieve

He was a ronin, a 20-year-old samurai without a lord or master to whom he could swear his loyalty. He wandered 17th-century Japan on *musha shugyō*—a samurai warrior's quest or pilgrimage. During his travels, he practiced and honed his skills as a swordsman without protection from his family or school. This was a very dangerous way of life and few samurai lasted long without the strength of a clan affiliation. It was not long before he entered a town and was challenged by the Yoshioka Clan to a duel by a warrior named Seijuro Yoshioka. Because of the ronin's youth, Yoshioka considered him an easy target. The contest was to be fought, not with razor-sharp samurai swords, but with wooden blades. The fight was not to the death but was to be decided by a single blow.

The two warriors faced each other. Yoshioka was an experienced samurai, much older than the younger ronin and expected to win. Yoshioka took his opening stance, with his wooden sword outstretched in an offensive posture, and stood perfectly still. The ronin took up a similar stance, also remaining still. Time passed. Neither man moved, but kept to their form, intently focused on each other. A slight breeze blew by. Yoshioka turned his eyes for one millisecond, distracted for the moment. The young ronin pounced with the swiftness of an eagle. His attack was precise, and in that split second, the duel was over. The ronin's wooden sword broke Yoshioka's arm, winning the match with one strike. Yoshioka was so humiliated that he retired, shed his sword, and became a monk.

Miyamoto Musashi was the young ronin in this story, and he became Japan's greatest swordsman. Raised by Zen Buddhist monks, he trained to be an expert in the martial arts and in the spiritual and moral dimensions of life. As he learned, he became both an educated man and a feared warrior. He is the author of the classic book of leadership, philosophy, tactics and strategy titled *A Book of Five Rings* (Victor Harris [translator], Gramercy,

May 28, 1988 [first published 1643]). Musashi's life-story is an extraordinary saga about self-mastery, focus and visualization. At the age of 13, he won his first duel and became a swordsman. He never lost a duel, and after over 60 victories, he became a legend in Japan. He was a man of intense focus who visualized his movements so perfectly, and performed them so swiftly, that there seemed to be no gap between thought and action. Moving at the speed of thought was a powerful skill that Musashi mastered. In another duel, his most famous, against a sword-wielding samurai named Kojiro, he defeated his skilled opponent using only a wooden oar.

> ### Lessons from Miyamoto Musashi
>
> "There is nothing outside of yourself that can ever enable you to get better, stronger, richer, quicker, or smarter. Everything is within. Everything exists.
> Seek nothing outside of yourself."

More than just a warrior, Musashi won his duels with focus and strategy as much as his skill as a swordsman. All his life he focused on self-improvement and personal growth. He was a deep thinker, a poet and a *sumi-e* (Zen brush ink painting) artist. This artistic talent may have been a key to his ability to visualize. He believed that to truly understand the art of leadership and strategy, you must hone your skills in various arts, and you must see it in your mind's eye. "Polish your wisdom: learn public justice, distinguish between good and evil, study the Ways of different arts one by one," Musashi recommended. The "Way" refers to the samurai moral values that stressed loyalty, sincerity, frugality, martial arts mastery and honor until death. "When you cannot be deceived by men, you will have realized the wisdom of strategy." Around 1645 AD, shortly before his death, he documented his teachings in five books, four of them titled after one of the four elements: *Earth* (knowledge of leadership and training to act); *Water* (knowledge of strategy, attitude and philosophy to think fluidly); *Fire* (knowledge of fighting methods and techniques to act decisively); and *Wind* (knowledge of his surroundings and the strategies of his opponents to act correctly). His fifth book, titled *Void*, deals with the mind and perceiving what is difficult to comprehend, executing each action according to the proper principles. Each book, although focused on sword fighting and war, is also a study of leadership and human philosophy.

A leader requires character to deal with the stress, uncertainties and the contradictions of conflict; the discipline and training to master the competencies of the profession; and the commitment to follow through and do whatever it takes to be honorable and right. Musashi's theme is that leaders must prepare, perceive, focus, and act. Musashi believed that your internal character, competencies and commitment drive you to succeed. Lacking these qualities hampers your ability to win. Negatives in each of these three categories can cause you to fail. Leaders study Musashi's writings to this day and his teachings have had a tremendous impact on the Japanese culture.

The critical lessons from Musashi are not about sword fighting but about leadership. Musashi believed in living by a set of simple principles to achieve mastery. He did not believe in a quick and easy road to success. The most important lessons he relates are that a leader benefits from habitual study; a clear focus; the ability to visualize; and the inner strength and discipline to follow through to overcome adversity. "The long sword seems heavy and unwieldy to everyone at first," Musashi wrote, "but everything is like that when you first take it up." Learning to become a better leader is like this. There are no easy paths.

To be a pathfinder and to know the way, a leader should work on visualization. Mental imagery can improve the performance of any skill. Visualization involves the ability to think through the steps to achieve the goal, reject the negative images of failure that spring up into your consciousness, and plan for the challenges that will always arise. If you can see your goal in your mind's eye and imagine the steps to realize it, then you are moving closer to achieving that aim. These mental workouts can help you improve your cognitive abilities. Focused imaging activates many of the same neural networks in your brain that enable the completion of the actual task. Jack Nicklaus, one of the most successful golfers in modern times, said that he practiced each shot in his mind before taking it. Musashi did a similar mental visualization during every duel. Seeing the goal in your mind's eye predisposes you to achieving that goal. This visualization is vital for those who lead others. The Bible, Proverbs 29, states "Where there is no vision, the people perish" and so it is when leading any team. The mental energy required to visualize the path and the destination is an important accelerant to success. Visualizing the challenges, crafting a mental image of the solution, seeing yourself calm and focused during a trying discussion, can prepare you for the genuine encounter. We expect our leaders to see the possibilities and prepare us for them, which is why leaders who can plan are so critical to any organization. As Napoleon Hill said: "What the mind can conceive and believe, it can achieve."

Visualization is more than daydreaming; it is daydreaming with a purpose. It is a precursor to action. Leaders think, visualize and then act. Like Musashi's ability to act with his sword at the speed of thought, a leader who can envision the destination and communicate a clear and simple vision so that others can see the path, has performed a powerful act of influence. Focused visualization is a form of mental rehearsal. Train your mind to focus on your goal, then see yourself accomplishing it. In essence, we are what we think, therefore use this tool to understand, conceptualize and grow. "In effective personal leadership," said leadership and time-management expert Dr. Steven Covey, "visualization and affirmation techniques emerge naturally out of a foundation of well thought through purposes and principles that become the center of a person's life." John Tukey (1915–2000), a famous American mathematician, credited with developing a host of mathematical algorithms and scientific advances, assisting in the design of the U-2 reconnaissance aircraft, and coining the computer term "bit," used visualization to see what others could not. Professor Tukey said: "The greatest value of a picture is when it forces us to notice what we never expected to see."

At this point in your journey, you have learned the importance of knowing yourself and of sharpening your purpose. As discussed in Chapters 1 and 2, you have visualized your purpose by creating a personal mind map, which is a simplified "thought picture." If you can now envisage a picture of leadership, this image can serve as another rally point along your journey. Can you visualize the components of your leadership? When you visualize, you create in your mind what you want to achieve, turning the invisible (thought) into the visible (action). Robin Sharma, a best-selling author and renowned leadership coach, said this about visualization: "Everything is created twice, first in the mind and then in reality."

Visualizing a model of leadership can help anyone become a better leader and is fundamental to conditioning your mind and heart to react properly, at the speed of thought, to any situation. To do this, leaders must know their purpose. Leaders requires the character to deal with the stress, uncertainties and contradictions of conflict; the discipline and training to master the competencies of their profession; and the commitment to follow through and do whatever it takes that is honorable and right to achieve a vision for the future. Musashi wrote of the ability to visualize and to "perceive that which cannot be seen with the eye" as one of a leader's greatest skills. Just as there are many paths to knowledge, or as Musashi said, "There are many ways to get to the top of the mountain," there are many images to describe leadership.

To communicate your vision of leadership, you should be able to see it in your mind's eye, just as Musashi could visualize the strike of his sword. The diagram titled "Your Leadership Compass" provides an example of a visualization of leadership. As an example, the compass, an essential tool for a pathfinder, provides a useful analogy to explain your leadership story to others. Having a vivid image of leadership will help you create a clear mental picture that can then become part of your reality. Your Leadership Compass is a mental image of the major components of leadership. Take time to study this illustration and then we will explore each of its components.

Visualization

When you visualize, you create in your mind what you want to achieve, turning the invisible (thought) into the visible (action). Visualizing a model of leadership can help anyone become a better leader and is fundamental to conditioning your mind and heart to react properly, at the speed of thought, to any situation.

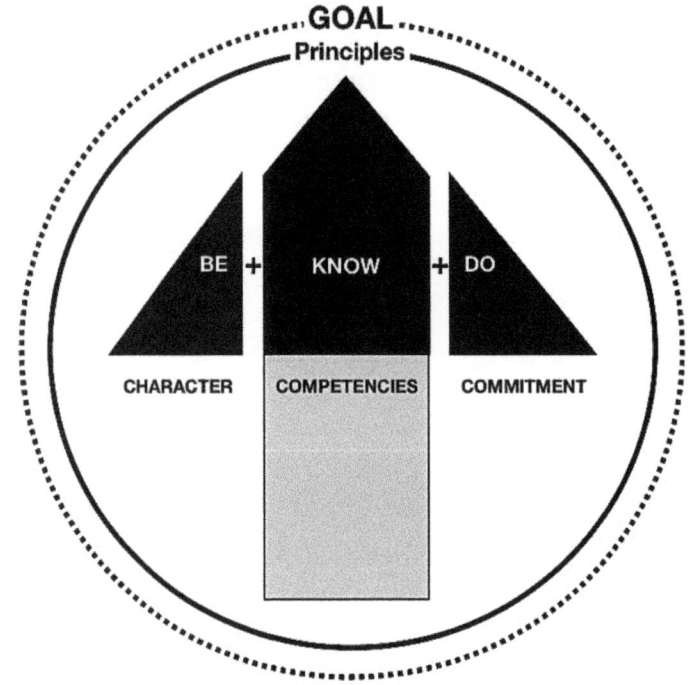

Your Leadership Compass

Your leadership compass is a visualization of your leadership.
Your GOAL is your objective.
Your PRINCIPLES are the overarching ideals you live by.
The three major components of leadership are:
CHARACTER (BE),
COMPETENCIES (KNOW), and COMMITMENT (DO).
Your leadership is at its best when your GOAL aligns
with your Principles and your Compass Arrow.

Your Immediate Goal

Leaders aim at achieving goals. Leaders that cannot achieve goals do not lead for long. Your goal can be self-designated or assigned by someone else. Set your path to achieve the goal. Visualize the steps necessary to bring your team to the desired destination. Leadership coach and author John Maxwell explains the relationship between goals and success as: "Your dream determines your goals. Your goals map out your actions. Your actions create results. And the results bring you success." He believes that goals need to be personal to be effective. If your goal is in line with your personal principles and values, you will not hesitate in a moment of crisis. Your leadership is most effective when you align your goal with the rest of your compass. If your goal is in a different direction than your principles, character, competencies and commitment, you will be misaligned and endanger achieving your goal.

Principles

In Chapter 2, you created a mind map that involved discovering your purpose, values, strengths, goals and legacy. Now you must go one step further and think about your guiding principles. By design, a compass needle points north. With the arrow pointing true, you can move confidently in any direction. Principles are similar. If you know what principles guide you, then you know when you are traveling in the right or wrong direction. The Merriam-Webster dictionary defines a principle as a comprehensive and fundamental law, doctrine or assumption. It is also defined as a fundamental truth or proposition that serves as the foundation for a system of beliefs, behavior, or a chain of reasoning. Principles help you designate true north and guide you on your leadership journey. Knowing your principles is another powerful way to know yourself and to always strive to be yourself. If you align your goals and principles, then this convergence can guide you to be a more consistent and compelling leader.

In his book, *The 7 Habits of Highly Effective People (Free Press, 1989)*, Dr. Stephen Covey defines a principle as "a natural law like gravity. It is different from a value. Values are subjective; principles are objective. Gravity… if you drop something, gravity controls." Covey uses the Law of the Harvest to explain how principles rule your life and all you do. On a farm, you quickly learn that you reap what you sow. If you sow wheat, you may grow wheat, but only if you work hard to water, weed and nurture your crop. Life is like that. You will reap what you sow. Want to grow a garden of flowers but do not like to garden? If you produce whatever you put your time, talent and energy into, then ignoring your garden will yield a bed full of dead and sickly plants. Consistently neglect your health and you will have medical problems. Want to write a book? Write a page each day and, in a year, you may have the basis of a novel. Routinely spend all of your earnings each month, and put nothing away in savings, and you will end up without a nest egg. Text on your mobile phone while you are driving, and you are likely to have an accident. Read books, learn, and improve your thinking; or only watch TV and surf the Internet and watch as your mind languishes. Preparation and study now, with the right nurturing, can grow into wisdom. The Law of the Harvest is unchangeable, immutable, and constant. It does not care about you. It is not fair, has no empathy, and is unforgiving. It is a principle of life: control the input and you improve the prospects for a positive outcome. If you dream big and do the work, you have a chance at achieving your desires, but it takes consistent, dedicated effort. Small actions, like taking the first step, can grow over time into greater rewards that will deliver you to your destination, but only if you keep on walking.

The Law of the Harvest

On a farm, you quickly learn that you reap what you sow. If you sow wheat, you may grow wheat, but only if you work hard to water, weed, and nurture your crop. Life is like that.

According to Covey, a principle, therefore, is a natural law. Natural laws are fundamental truths. They are absolute. They are cause and effect. If you break natural laws, like the law of gravity, it hurts you, unless for example, you plan to jump off the cliff with a parachute and pull the ripcord at the proper moment. Light and dark, water and fire, life and death are all examples of absolutes we live with and cannot change. Today, we do not like to think in terms of absolutes, but they are immutable. We think our technology can change all this, turn night into light, hot into cold, and sickness into health, but eventually, the natural law wins out. Learning to deal with the natural laws of life is the essence of becoming an adult.

What then are the natural laws of leadership? If principles are natural laws and self-evident, then what are the principles that should guide our leadership? Covey cites four natural laws of leadership that, according to him, transcend cultures and time. They are security, guidance, wisdom and power. Security is our sense of value, feelings, identity, personal strength and self-respect. Guidance is your life's bearing, the direction you take in life. Wisdom is the convergence of knowledge and experience. Power is the capacity to decide, act and follow through to accomplish something. According to Covey, if you understand these four principles, you can transform them into a powerful compass that will keep you on the right path to continue your leadership journey.

Leadership Principles

Leadership principles are your guiding rules or code of conduct.

Ray Dalio, a successful investor and the author of the best-selling book *Principles* (Simon & Schuster, 2017), says that he has three main principles in life: "Think for yourself to decide 1) what you want, 2) what is true, and 3) what you should do to achieve #1 in light of #2, and do that with humility and open-mindedness so you consider the best thinking available to you." He says that each one of us must determine our own principles, learning from our life's journey and every episode of leadership we experience.

In today's world, living by principles seems to have gone out of style. The principles declared by many colleges, for instance, are merely guidelines for behavior. There are some exceptions. At the United States Military Academy at West Point they teach cadets three general principles that are expected to guide graduates their entire life: Duty, Honor and Country. General Douglas MacArthur explained the impact of these principles in his famous speech at West Point in 1962.

> Those three hallowed words reverently dictate what you ought to be, what you can be, what you will be. They are your rallying point to build courage when courage seems to fail, to regain faith when there seems to be little cause for faith, to create hope when hope becomes forlorn… The code which those words perpetuate embraces the highest moral laws and will stand the test of any ethics or philosophies ever promulgated for the uplift of mankind. Its requirements are for the things that are right, and its restraints are from the things that are wrong.

Duty is the work you are responsible for. Honor is the conviction to do the right thing, even when no one is watching. Country is the concept of selfless service to defend the American Republic, to the point that you will sacrifice your life in its defense. This may work for the soldiers who attend West

Point, and there is much that anyone can learn from these principles, but can they be of value for everyone else? Can we somehow craft a list of leadership principles from understanding such varied sources as Musashi, Covey, Dalio and West Point?

Leadership principles, to be a fundamental truth, cannot solely be a list of values, but must be your guiding rules or code of conduct. That most people do not have principles that they can articulate, highlights the fact that their thinking is vague, and that at the moment of decision, without a compass to guide them, they may go astray, choosing the easier wrong instead of the harder right. The person with firm principles will act correctly in the decisive moment, not straying from the correct path. The time taken to understand your principles, the fundamental truths that guide your life, is a worthy undertaking.

The Most Important Freedom

The most important freedom in life is the ability to think and decide for yourself.

If we look at Musashi's principles, there is an overarching theme of the value of time, both in the ability to act at the speed of thought and to recognize that every human is mortal and therefore has a limited amount of time to grow, learn, and realize his or her fullest potential. Covey's comprehensive idea is the value of knowledge and experience and subsequently transforming that into wisdom. Dalio's comprehensive concept is for the individual to think and to choose. He expressed this choice as the greatest virtue. West Point's Duty, Honor and Country is a timeless set of principles that have guided military leaders to uphold the values of a free government.

The most important freedom in life is the ability to think and decide for yourself. Your greatest challenge and gift in life is to adopt your own set of principles that can become your "North Star." If your goals and principles are not in alignment, then the inconsistencies between your words and actions will eventually become apparent to those you lead. You will be perceived as a leader who believes one thing, but does something quite different.

Consider the following as an example set of personal principles that can assist you in creating your own list. These principles are best put into a single sentence that expresses the intent of the value and links it to an action. Imagine these principles and how they might guide your life.

1. *I love others as I love myself:* Love requires you to have empathy and compassion, to think beyond yourself, to place yourself in another's shoes, and understand how your actions will affect others and the team you lead. This example of principle encapsulates the "golden rule" of doing unto others as we would like others to do unto us.

2. *I live with virtue, putting service before self:* Virtue beckons you to do the right thing, to listen to your conscience and your inner voice that tells you the difference between right and wrong. You can lead by putting self before service, or service before self. Which kind of leader would you rather follow? Living with this attitude and putting service before self can be a powerful example that will influence people.

3. *I seek wisdom, the combination of knowledge and experience, and am a lifelong learner:* If you focus time and energy to gain knowledge and experience, and reflect on how they meld to create wisdom, you can help yourself and others along your leadership path.

4. *I value every moment and want to make the most of the limited time I have to make a difference:* Time reminds you that the clock is always ticking, that life is short, and that we all should make the most of every precious moment. Steve Jobs, the genius developer and cofounder of Apple Inc., once said about time: "My favorite things in life don't cost any money. It's really clear that the most precious resource we all have is time."

Writing a list of principles is not a wasted effort in philosophy. Think of the insights you will experience once you list your guiding principles. If you practice your principles, and live by them, they will help form habits that become the scaffolding of your future. This idea is represented in the adage of sowing and reaping. Ralph Waldo Emerson is credited with saying, "Sow an action, reap a habit. Sow a habit, reap a character. Sow a character, reap a destiny." If you want to reap a destiny and create a future, choose the principles that will guide your actions in life. Think and decide for yourself. Principles are not just "dust and air;" they can be the azimuth that directs your actions at the moment of decision when you must balance between right and wrong, between your personal benefit over the benefit of a greater good. If your principles are sound, they become a compass that will point you in the right direction to guide your decision-making. Don't worry that you are not schooled in philosophy. Marcus Aurelius, ancient Rome's great emperor-philosopher, put it this way: "No role is so well suited to philosophy as the one you happen to be in right now."

Reap a Destiny

If you want to reap a destiny, choose the principles that will guide your actions in life.

What are your guiding leadership principles? Write them down, on the next page, and include a short, one-line explanation of what they mean to you. Initially, do not try to word them perfectly. If you close your eyes, center yourself, and think deeply about the principles that should guide your life, the words will manifest themselves.

My Guiding Principles Are:

1._____

_____

_____

_____

2._____

_____

_____

_____

3._____

_____

_____

_____

4._____

_____

_____

Character

Study the diagram labeled "Your Leadership Compass" and imagine the needle that keeps your leadership "on course" is comprised of three components: Character, Competencies and Commitment. The interaction of character, competencies and commitment, when aligned with principles, maintains your heading. Character keeps actions and words in line with principles. Character is the bedrock of your reputation and the foundation of your leadership. The Oxford dictionary defines character as the mental and moral qualities distinctive to an individual. It is the ability to know and do the right thing, all the time. Exemplary character is about being truthful, doing what is right even when it is hard, looking out for the common good, keeping promises and earning trust. Character matters. Reverend Martin Luther King implored us not to judge people "by the color of their skin but by the content of their character." He knew that character was a decisive attribute.

Content of Their Character

"I look to a day when people will not be judged by the color of their skin, but by the content of their character."
Martin Luther King, Jr.

Authors Chris Brady and Orrin Woodward, in their bestselling book *Launching a Leadership Revolution, Mastering the Five Levels of Influence* (Business Plus, 2007), reported: "nobody lacking in character will succeed in a meaningful way... character includes honesty, integrity, courage, power values based on absolute truths, faith, a humble spirit, patience with others, discipline and self-mastery." A manipulator may succeed for a while, but eventually a leader without character sows only sorrow. Character includes being a good follower and understanding the dictum of Aristotle to his young pupil, Alexander: a leader must learn to obey before he can lead, and must learn to follow before they can command.

A great test of character is to watch how people treat other people when they believe that person has no power or status. Pauline Esther "Popo" Phillips, who began the famous "Dear Abby" column in print and on radio in the 1950s, famously said: "The best index to a person's character is how he treats people who can't do him any good, and how he treats people who can't fight back." Abraham Lincoln, the 16th president of the United States, revealed his test for character by declaring: "Nearly all men can stand adversity, but if you want to test a man's character, give him power." Your character builds your reputation. Reputation is like a bank account and character is the daily investment that can pay off later with interest. Although reputation can be hyped, character is observed and built with deeds. Lincoln keenly expressed the difference between character and reputation by saying: "Character is like a tree and reputation like a shadow. The shadow is what we think of it; the tree is the real thing." As the real thing, character can inspire confidence and build trust. Trust often becomes the "oil" that reduces the friction that arises in the execution of any challenging task or project.

> ### Exemplary Character
>
> **Character is the mental and moral qualities distinctive to an individual. It is the ability to know and do the right thing, all the time. Exemplary character is about being truthful, doing what is right even when it is hard, looking out for the common good, keeping promises and earning trust.**

Trust is something that all leaders want and need. Everyone desires to be trusted, but do you know what trust is? If you want to earn the trust of those who follow you, a clear definition is required. What is your definition of trust? Think about this and write down your definition of trust on the next page.

My Definition of Trust

Trust is _____

_____

_____

_____

_____

_____

_____

_____

_____

_____

_____

_____

_____

_____

_____

_____

_____

_____

_____

_____

_____

_____

_____

Your definition of trust must be one you believe in. I define trust as consistent, consecutive and coherent action observed. Words equal action. It is not what you say, it is what you say and then what you do that engenders trust. If you tell me that you will be in the office every day at 8:30 a.m., but consistently stroll in after 9 a.m., your words and actions are in conflict. I will not trust you to be in the office when you tell me you will be there, be it at 8:30 a.m. or any other time. Trust is saying what you mean and doing what you say. If you lie, cheat and steal, it is impossible for anyone to trust you and you will earn a reputation as a person of poor character. If you do what you say, consistently, consecutively, and coherently, people will learn to trust you.

Reservoir of Trust

Character is a combination of positive values that becomes your reservoir of trust.

Character is the combination of positive values that become your reservoir of trust. General Norman Schwarzkopf, the American general who successfully led the United States Armed Forces in Operation *Desert Storm* and was responsible for the strategy used to win the war in Iraq, believed that character is the most important element of leadership. "Leadership is a potent combination of strategy and character," Schwarzkopf declared. "But if you must be without one, be without the strategy." A good, moral character, therefore, is a vital element of your leadership. To make a banking analogy, every time you act properly, you make a deposit into your trust account. Even if no one is watching, doing the right thing increases your confidence and strengthens your character. Every time you act irresponsibly, you make a withdrawal. Eventually, if you make too many withdrawals, your character is bankrupt. There is no substitute for character. Once you ruin your character by intolerable acts, and stain your reputation, it is nearly impossible to recover. Recall the rich and famous people you have read about, watched on television, or learned about on the Internet, who have lost their reputations over scandalous deeds. Most thought they were so famous or powerful that the rules of character did not apply to them. In all probability, they did not have a defined set of principles to guide them, and they did not understand that their character was their most valuable asset.

In the United States Army, there is a saying: "An officer is always on parade." This means that a leader is constantly observed by the soldiers, be it on or off duty. Similarly, in every walk of life, your team members observe everything you do as a leader. They hear everything you say. Your words and actions matter. If you think you will get away with minor infractions, guess again. When you break the rules, someone will invariably uncover it and, when one person knows, eventually everyone will. Leaders are always on parade, being observed and judged by those they lead. Your character becomes your armor and protection against negative thoughts and actions. It is about doing the right thing, especially when you think no one is watching. You must act to develop your own character and consider positive improvements as deposits into your character account.

Competencies

Before you can lead others, you must develop yourself. Without actual expertise, can you really know what you are doing? Proficiency matters. No one wishes to follow an incompetent leader. Every leadership role has different requirements, but all require competence in leadership and technical skills. How can you enforce standards if you cannot do the work yourself? If you do not have competency in your core tasks, your people will be frustrated with your lack of knowledge. There is no faster way to lose the respect of your team than to be unable to do the job you expect others to perform. People will rapidly lose confidence in your leadership if they believe that you are incompetent in the tasks you expect them to perform. To be competent, you should have the necessary abilities, knowledge, and skills to execute your assigned tasks and missions successfully. If you have no idea how to do the work that you direct others to do, you are a failing leader and a hypocrite. Take time to learn. Make a list of the basic skills that you must learn to lead your team. You must be competent if you expect people to follow you.

To lead to your highest potential, you need the skills required to get the job done—not only to lead the team, but to set the example and show that you can do the work. You must be competent at the essential skills of your team members in order to be able to teach others. Teaching is an important aspect of leadership, as one of the key responsibilities of a leader is to grow the next generation of leaders. Effective leaders are competent in both people skills and technical tasks. In the military, this is referred to as being "technically and tactically proficient." You are technically proficient if you can perform your job to the established standard. Being tactically proficient means that you know when and how to use these skills to accomplish the mission. Without these skills, you will not gain the trust, confidence, and loyalty of your team members. For first line leaders, the skills required involve the work you ask others to do. For strategic leaders, these skills involve higher-order competencies such as decision-making, planning and communication. Fail to master the essential skills at your specific level of leadership and you will soon lose the faith and confidence of those who follow you. If you don't know the business, it's hard to lead others to succeed. If all leadership is by example, then show that you can do the work and you will earn the respect of your team.

> ### Being Competent
>
> To be competent, develop the abilities, knowledge and skills to do your assigned tasks and missions successfully. If you cannot do what you tell others to do, you are a failing leader and a hypocrite.

Every leader requires general leadership skills that focus on the human aspects of motivating, communicating, planning, critical thinking, problem solving, delegating tasks and teaching. Of these, communicating by the spoken and written word is a primary leadership skill. Communication is the key to all human relationships. If you cannot communicate, you cannot lead. The more proficient you become at communication, the higher are your chances of success. Communication involves both receiving and transmitting. To be effective communicators, leaders benefit more from listening (receiving) than from talking (transmitting). "Listen more and talk less" is a useful maxim for any person, especially a new and inexperienced leader.

If it is impossible to lead effectively without some technical expertise, then leaders must seek every opportunity to grow and learn. In today's age of technological acceleration, being competent and up to date at technical tasks is vital to understand the context and depth to be poised to make timely and accurate decisions. No one wants to follow someone who cannot decide, or consistently makes wrong decisions. You do not have to be the expert at everything, but if you cannot do the job, find someone to teach you and earn a proficiency that will raise your competency and inspire your team members. To be competent at their technical tasks, new leaders must invest the time and energy to improve and eventually demonstrate the basic competencies of their job. This is accomplished by first understanding what skills you must have and then diligently working to master them. Developing your competence will boost your self-confidence, increase your influence and reinforce your credibility. Seeking self-improvement that benefits the group will gain the respect of your team members. Take on the motto of Musashi: "Today is victory over yourself of yesterday; tomorrow is your victory over lesser men." Become a lifelong leader, learn to be tactically and technically proficient, and your team members will follow you because you will have become their pathfinder.

> ## Technical Competencies
>
> Every leader requires technical skills that show they can do the work. You do not have to be the expert at everything, but if you cannot do the job, find someone to teach you and earn a proficiency that will raise your competency and inspire your team members.

A short story about the importance of competencies: In my first assignment as an officer in the United States Army, I was assigned to the 3rd Battalion, 32nd Armored Regiment, in Friedberg, Germany. This was at the height of the Cold War. My experience in the Army to this point included four years of education and training at the United States Military Academy at West Point, Airborne and Ranger schools, and a four-month tank platoon leaders training course at Fort Knox, Kentucky. I was as ready as any wet-behind-the-ears 2nd Lieutenant could be and eager for the challenge of leading my first platoon. I knew that I was not proficient in the tasks required of a tank commander, as I had not trained long enough to gain any degree of mastery. On my first day, my senior leader, the Company Commander, told me his intent was to assign me to lead the 3rd Tank Platoon. He had reservations, however, as the Platoon Sergeant, who was currently in charge, did not want an officer assigned to his platoon. The Platoon Sergeant, Larry Stipe, felt he was doing fine as the "Acting Platoon Leader" and he did not relish the chore of training a brand-new 2nd Lieutenant. Platoon Sergeant Stipe had been leading the five tanks of the 3rd Platoon for nearly a year without an officer in charge. The Company Commander went on to tell me that Stipe had a reputation as a no-nonsense tank sergeant, an expert tank soldier and an exceptional leader. I told the Company Commander that I understood the challenge and I would make it work. He smiled and assigned me as the Platoon Leader of 3rd Platoon.

The next day, I met my Platoon Sergeant. I found Stipe in the motor pool with the soldiers of the platoon hard at work conducting maintenance on their tanks. Stipe was wearing green mechanic coveralls and covered in dirt and grease. I will never forget this first meeting. As Platoon Leader, my job was to lead the platoon, but here I was meeting an experienced non-commissioned officer who had been successfully doing this for over a year. I recognized that he did not need me. If I was to be successful, I had to show him how I could add to the team. I offered him my hand and said: "Platoon Sergeant, I have been assigned as the Platoon Leader of the 3rd Platoon. I don't know much about tanks or leading a tank platoon. If you teach me, I promise to listen and learn." Stipe looked me over for a long moment while I stood in front of him with my hand extended. The rest of the soldiers stopped working and looked on, curious how this encounter would turn out.

Individual and Team Leadership Levels

Experienced leaders know that it is not enough to raise just individual skills. Great leaders raise the team level as well.

Finally, Stipe smiled and laughed: "Okay Sir, I've been waiting for a lieutenant like you. If you want to learn, I'll teach you." He shook my hand and directed me to report back to the motor pool in mechanic's coveralls. I obeyed and "went to school" for the next three weeks under Stipe's watchful eye. He taught me more about tanks, leadership, and being a platoon leader than I ever imagined. I learned never to underestimate the value of an expert instructor. Mentors are invaluable. To this day, I consider that experience as the most important lesson I received on the value of learning and leading. An outstanding leader is skilled at teaching and raising the skill level of individuals and the team. Exceptional leaders, like Platoon Sergeant Larry Stipe, are also great coaches and know how to lead and influence their leader. I may have had the rank and authority, but Stipe was the expert. He led and trained me. We came to an agreement where I led the platoon, but he ran its day-to-day operations. This relationship helped make our platoon one of the best in the battalion, in maintenance readiness levels, tank gunnery, and tactics. Leadership is not about rank or authority, it is about influence. Stipe was a leader and a teacher. The wisest move I ever made was to admit my lack of experience and enlist his support to teach me. It amazes me to this day that I had the good luck to figure this out early in my career.

Train Well

Navy Seals are paying tribute to Archilochus, the ancient Greek philosopher (680–645 BC), when they say:
"When you are under pressure, you don't rise to the occasion, you sink to the level of your training."

Experienced leaders know that it is not enough to raise individual skills. Outstanding leaders raise the team level as well. Just as individuals can increase their skill level, each team has a leadership and skill level that the leader must understand, raise and nurture. Leaders do this by thoughtful and focused teaching (providing the theory that reinforces knowledge), training (exercising the task successfully), coaching (personalized and customized one-on-one performance-based teaching), and mentoring (relation-based education by an experienced leader). As Archilochus, a revered and famous Greek poet-warrior who composed poetry between battles, revered by the ancient Greeks as one of their most brilliant authors, and who lived from 680 to 645 BC, said: "We don't rise to the level of our expectations, we fall to the level of our training." Take time to train your team to a high level of performance and they can exceed expectations. Focus this training on what the team does, not individual skills. Be the exception and rather than complain that there is no time or money to train, find ways to do this. Challenge your team and set high standards. If input impacts output, what you invest in your team can pay dividends. For me, Platoon Sergeant Larry Stipe was my Archilochus, and he took the time to train me and raised my level of leadership by increasing my technical and tactical proficiency.

Commitment

Commitment is desire and passion dedicated to a cause or activity. The leader's level of commitment to persevere and secure the goal can inspire others to adopt the same level of dedication. On the contrary, a leader with little commitment can inspire indifference among the team. Without commitment, you seldom start, and you never finish. Without commitment, small obstacles appear big and you do not overcome the barriers that block your path.

A pathfinder must have a strong sense of commitment to move forward into the unknown. It is easier to stay safe at home, or follow someone else's path, rather than blaze new trails into uncharted territory. Imagine the personal commitment it took for astronauts Neil Armstrong, Michael Collins and Edwin "Buzz" Aldrin to be part of the Apollo 11 mission and be the first humans to land on the Moon. These three were the best astronauts America could produce. They were men of outstanding character. They had extraordinary competence and had been repeatedly tested in dangerous and intense situations and training. On May 6, 1968, at Ellington Air Force Base near the Manned Spacecraft Center (MSC) in Houston, Armstrong was conducting a training flight of the lunar-landing research vehicle, an aircraft meant to simulate the lunar module. Armstrong piloted the aircraft high into the sky when he lost all control due to a systems malfunction. The test vehicle's instrumentation did not provide any warning of the pending malfunction. Then, the vehicle suddenly burst into flames. As the test lunar lander hurtled to the ground, Armstrong had only seconds to decide what to do. He ejected 200 feet above the ground with no time to spare, just before the lander crashed and exploded in a ball of fire. The crash investigation found that a helium pressure leak caused a failure of the attitude thrusters. If this happened on the Moon, everyone in the lander would have been killed. This close call proved Armstrong's excellence at decision-making and competence. The crew of Apollo 11 were ready, but the risks were significant as the lunar module accident indicated. No human had ever done this before. Commitment was decisive. Without the commitment of the crew, the entire team at National Aeronautics and Space Administration (NASA), and the political leaders in the United States, to accomplish the mission and be the first to land on the Moon, all the character and competence in the galaxy would not get them there.

Undaunted by setbacks, the commitment to land a man on the Moon held firm. The Apollo 11 mission, which began with a picture-perfect launch of a massive Saturn V rocket on July 16, 1969, from NASA's Kennedy Space Center's Launch Complex 39A, blasted the three astronauts toward the Moon. On their television sets, the people of America and the world watched in awe as the crew sent video updates back to Earth. Four days of travel finally brought Armstrong, Aldrin, and Collins to the Moon. Their rocket ship consisted of a combination of a "command module" and a "lunar module" system. On July 20, Armstrong and Aldrin, now inside the lunar module, code-named the Eagle, separated from the lunar orbiter, fired their rocket engines, and sped down toward the chalk-white surface of the Moon. Collins waited alone in the command module, code-named Columbia, and maintained radio communications with the Eagle and NASA's Mission Control headquarters in Houston, Texas. Everyone seemed to hold their collective breath and pray that all would go well.

Commitment

Commitment is desire and passion dedicated to a cause or activity.
It is your level of enthusiasm and devotion to a goal.
Without commitment, you seldom start, and you never finish.

The descent of the lunar module went according to plan, but as the Eagle got closer to the designated landing zone, the navigational computer system flashed an error code. One can only imagine what was going through Armstrong's mind as this alarm flashed on the tiny screen. Only a year before, he was nearly killed in a similar situation attempting to land the simulated lunar module. This time, however, there was no escape. He and Aldrin could not eject from the lunar module, and besides, there was no place to eject to. They needed the Eagle to survive. Armstrong had to make a very rapid decision.

Armstrong radioed Mission Control. Houston told him that the experts at NASA thought the malfunction was an error due to an overloaded circuit. There was no time to verify if their hunch was correct. The final decision to abort or continue rested solely with Armstrong, the lunar module commander. Armstrong decided to continue the mission and Aldrin was in complete agreement. The spacecraft's landing system was set on automatic pilot to bring the lunar module to the landing site, a section of the Moon called Sea of Tranquility, but looking out the small window of the craft, Armstrong could see large boulders covering the planned landing area. If the lunar module hit one of those boulders, it could break a landing leg and the mission would end in disaster with two American astronauts killed, or if they survived, stranded on the Moon until their oxygen ran out. There was no possibility of rescue and no second chance. Armstrong knew that the lunar module had just enough fuel to land on the surface with very little to spare for additional maneuver. He checked the fuel gauge, looked at Aldrin, and decided. A less committed leader might have aborted the mission, but not Armstrong. He took over the controls, disconnected the auto landing system, and manually maneuvered the Eagle around the boulders to a safe landing spot. At 3:17 p.m. EST on July 20, 1969, the Eagle safely touched down in the Sea of Tranquility. Armstrong subsequently transmitted that now famous transmission to NASA: "Houston, the Eagle has landed."

Imagine if you had to make the decisions that Neil Armstrong, Buzz Aldrin and Michael Collins faced during the Apollo 11 mission to the Moon in July 1969. The technology that took American astronauts to the Moon was nascent.

The computing power of the command and lunar modules was only 2K, less than what we use in a musical greeting card today. Looking at a model of the lunar module, it has the appearance of a tin can, with some electronics, a rocket motor and four legs. The external siding of the lunar module was paper thin in many places. The most significant power of the Apollo mission was in the human power of the leader and the team, not the equipment they operated. Armstrong, Aldrin and Collins, along with the entire NASA team back on Earth, had the character, competence and commitment to get the job done. The entire team's unwavering dedication was paramount, particularly the commitment of Armstrong at the decisive moment. Commitment, therefore, is about action. It is the difference between talking and doing. Without the driving commitment to succeed, Apollo 11's crew would never have been the first to land on the Moon and safely return to Earth.

The difference between involvement and commitment is primary and strikingly clear in the story of Apollo 11. Involved means you are interested, but not fully engaged. You are essentially a "tourist," not responsible for success or failure. When you are committed, you are the pathfinder, accepting responsibility for success and failure. You are no longer just interested; you are dedicated to accomplishing the mission. Abraham Lincoln stated that "commitment is what turns a promise into reality." Commitment requires personal investment and strongly identifying with the cause. John Adams, a key patriot, champion of American liberty during the American Revolution and America's 2nd President, in a letter to his wife Abigail, said: "There are only two creatures of value on the face of the earth: those with the commitment, and those who require the commitment of others." Adams later said in an address before the Continental Congress: "Live or die; sink or swim; survive or perish; I am committed to this Declaration of Independence. I am committed, and if God wills it, I am ready to die that this nation may be free." Adams clearly understood, and more importantly, lived the difference between involvement and commitment.

The Difference Between Involvement and Commitment

Involved means you are interested, but not fully engaged. You are essentially a "tourist," not responsible for success or failure. When you are committed, you are the pathfinder, accepting responsibility for success and failure. You are no longer just interested; you are dedicated to accomplishing the mission.

Ask yourself this question: "Why would anyone follow me?" Reflecting on what you have learned thus far, you can begin to answer this important question. First, you are learning to know yourself, the first step in raising your leadership awareness. Second, you have explored your purpose, a sign that you have decided on a direction. Third, you can visualize a model of leadership that describes your principles, character, competencies, and commitment and can see this model in your mind's eye. This is a powerful convergence of ideas. Leadership is difficult, but we can learn and improve our skills. "It may seem difficult at first," Musashi warns us, "but everything is difficult at first." Armed with this knowledge, in the next chapter, you will develop a personal definition of leadership.

Chapter Summary

1. Goals can be temporary, but principles are timeless. The most important freedom in life is the ability to think and decide for yourself. Your significant challenge and gift in life is to adopt your own set of principles that can become your "North Star."

2. When you align your goals and principles, you become a more consistent and compelling leader.

3. Character, competencies and commitment: A leader requires the character to deal with the stress, uncertainties and contradictions of conflict; the discipline and training to learn the competencies of their profession; and the commitment to follow through and do whatever it takes that is honorable and right to achieve a vision for the future.

4. Character: Character is "the mental and moral qualities distinctive to an individual." It is the ability to know and do the right thing all the time.

5. Competencies: Every leader requires technical skills that show they can do the work. The mastery of specific professional skills is fundamental to leadership.

6. Commitment: Commitment is your ability to accomplish the task and accept responsibility for success and failure. Commitment helps you to start, persevere and accomplish.

7. Visualization is a critical leadership ability. Visualization involves the ability to think through the steps to achieve the goal, reject the negative images of failure that spring up into the consciousness, and plan ahead for the challenges that will always arise.

A Personal Definition of Leadership

All Understanding Begins with Definition

True leaders are rare. Heraclitus, an ancient Greek philosopher who was a native of the city of Ephesus and practiced philosophy before the time of Socrates, understood the extraordinary nature of leadership in battle: "Out of every 100 men, ten shouldn't even be there, 80 are just targets, nine are the real fighters, and we are lucky to have them, for they make the battle. Ah, but the one, one is a warrior, and he will bring the others back."

How can you learn to unlock your potential and become an effective, or even an extraordinary, leader? There are scores of bosses, numerous managers and supervisors, but few genuine leaders. Many consider leadership to comprise intangible qualities that are impossible to reproduce. Therefore, most organizations default to creating and developing managers. Managers follow the process and can teach the process to others. One reason for this default setting is that leadership is difficult to define and harder to develop. People have been studying and teaching leadership since civilization began. Leadership is an art, not a science, and therefore it defies a simple explanation or definition. As an art, leadership is unique to every individual; there is no single, codified definition for all.

We can, however, define leadership on a personal level. Extraordinary leaders develop a personal definition of leadership, and then live by their definition. They are extraordinary because they have taken time to study leadership and understand the dynamics of the art. Their personal definition of leadership becomes their distinctive pledge and affirmation, a rule that they learn to live by. Aristotle, in his work entitled *Nicomachean Ethics*, described leadership as a dynamic comparison between human virtues that are universal and constant, and human actions that are variable and change with the situation. Aristotle believed that leaders must understand the principles of leadership to become effective leaders and then apply them to the ever-changing leadership landscape. To do this, emerging leaders must be broadly trained and educated.

The One

There are scores of bosses, numerous managers and supervisors, but few genuine leaders. Extraordinary leaders develop a personal definition of leadership and then live by their definition.

In an excellent article by David L. Cawthon, "Aristotle on Leadership," (*St. Croix Review*. 2001) the author states: "Without question, the philosophical insights of Aristotle have made a considerable impact upon our current understanding of leadership. Of all the philosophers who emerged from this golden age of Greek history, along with Socrates and Plato, he is among those who have been most influential in the formation of our understanding of leadership." Aristotle believed that the roots of leadership are *ethos* (values), *pathos* (human emotion), and *logos* (reason and logic), and that experience mattered. He famously told his pupil, a young Macedonian prince, that he would never learn to lead until he first learned to follow. Aristotle was expressing the belief that the qualities of a good follower were, in fact, preparation for good leadership. Aristotle's teachings must have had an impact as his pupil, Alexander, for he rose in leadership from the lands of northern Greece to become the leader of the greatest empire of his time.

The leadership exemplified by Alexander the Great in governing his vast empire differs vastly from what any of us will experience, but all leaders will face contemporary leadership challenges of their own. Leadership is reliant on context and changes with the conditions. As you grow in leadership, and move to ever-increasing roles of responsibility and complexity, your leadership environment will vary. If you lead in the same way, in every situation, you are mistaking art for science. Applying only one method or tenet of leadership will not be successful. The artful leader knows that there is no "one way" to lead; there are no static leadership situations. Leadership unfolds within a dynamic flow of people, emotions, actions, and chance—and the clock is always ticking. The leader must understand and survey the situation carefully. As a pathfinder studies the ravines, hills and rivers of a territory before embarking on a journey, a successful leader reads the human terrain before acting. The leader must consider people's goals, values, emotions and the power relationships within their team. As Musashi noted, there are many ways to get to the top of the mountain. A leader must scrutinize multiple paths and select the one that best accomplishes the team's goal at the least cost in resources. Most leaders fail to take the time to do this analysis of their human assets.

The Human Terrain

As a pathfinder who studies the ravines, hills and rivers of a territory before embarking on a journey, a successful leader reads the human terrain before acting.

Since the days of Heraclitus, philosophers and teachers have been unable to nail down a single definition for effective leadership behavior. This is as it should be. There is no simple recipe for leadership. Leadership is multifaceted and complex, yet achievable when the character, competencies and commitment of the leader are in harmony. Creating your own personal definition of leadership enhances that harmony. Someone else's definition should not be your own personal definition. A quick review of several definitions of leadership may inspire and help you to develop your own.

Leadership is Action: Leaders make things happen. Leadership is about getting teams to get things done and achieving goals. Peter Drucker, author and leadership expert, believed: "Leadership is defined by results not attributes." Leadership is the highest form of action in that it mobilizes the power of teams to accomplish more than any individual could do alone. A great misunderstanding about leadership is that leadership is about position. Donald McGannon, the chairman of the Westinghouse Broadcasting Company during the formative years of television in the 20th century said: "Leadership is an action, not a position." McGannon led the way in dropping cigarette commercials from television in an era when they were both profitable and popular. He understood that actions speak louder than words and believed that television had a social responsibility to pursue what Aristotle would have viewed as virtue. McGannon's leadership on cigarette advertising, and his leadership concerning social responsibility in the media, is credited with helping curb cigarette addiction.

Action

"Leadership is an action, not a position."
Donald McGannon

Leadership is Purpose: Leaders harness the developing passions of their team members to a purpose. Leaders survey the situation, learn the path, and with foresight, can plan, prepare and act to impel their team to seize opportunities and achieve goals. Successful leaders learn to sense the developing passions of their team and harness this spirit to a purpose. Jack Canfield, an American author, motivational speaker, corporate trainer, entrepreneur and co-author of the *Chicken Soup for the Soul* series, said: "If you can tune into your purpose and really align with it, setting goals so that your vision is an expression of that purpose, then life flows much more easily." Thomas Carlyle, the 19th-century British historian and author who wrote about leaders and leadership, famously said: "The person without a purpose is like a ship without a rudder." The question you should ask is: "Does my ship have a rudder?" If your purpose is to land on the Moon, then do everything it takes to land on the Moon. Where there is no spirit of purpose, successful leaders generate it.

Purpose

"The person without a purpose is like a ship without a rudder."
Thomas Carlyle

Leadership is Motivation: A leader motivates people and teams to action. Motivation is the ability to direct persistent effort to achieve a goal. Motivational leaders inspire and direct people to achieve. Theodore Roosevelt motivated those around him by reminding people to "Believe you can and you're halfway there." Motivation requires the ability to communicate by word and deed. Leaders who can impel people to be more than they thought they could be, and to work together as a team, possess a powerful ability. To do this, the best leaders know what motivates the people they lead. This is not a simple task, as humans are complex, but it starts with the ability of the leader to listen and learn. Alexander the Great, who by the age of 30 created one of the largest empires of the ancient world, inspired those he led by saying: "There is nothing impossible to him who will try," and then leading by example to make the seemingly impossible happen.

Motivation

"The greatest leader is not necessarily the one who does the greatest things. He is the one that gets the people to do the greatest things."
President Ronald Reagan

If a leader can learn the team's motivations, then the leader can address the desires and needs of the team members. The personal motivation of the members of a team will drive their individual actions. If a leader can unite those motivations to work toward the accomplishment of the team's goals, then the leader increases the team's probability of success. President Ronald Reagan, who excelled as a leader and communicator, believed: "The greatest leader is not necessarily the one who does the greatest things. He is the one that gets the people to do the greatest things."

Leadership is Trust: Trust is the cornerstone of all leadership. To trust is to join in spirit. Leaders need followers, otherwise they are merely managers. Author, speaker, and mega-successful entrepreneur Seth Godin put it this way: "Earn trust, earn trust, earn trust. Then you can worry about the rest." Dr. Stephen Covey wrote: "Trust is the highest form of human motivation because it brings out the very best in people." In his book, *The Speed of Trust: The One Thing That Changes Everything* (Simon and Schuster, 2006), Covey defines trust as confidence. "The opposite of that (confidence)—distrust—is suspicion." There is a truism that it only takes one lie to make you a liar or distrust someone who lied to you, and that honesty may not always pay, but lying always costs. Earning trust, therefore, is a critical investment in leadership that every leader must understand. If the leader is cowardly, dishonest, or undependable, the team will reflect those failings. If the leader is courageous, honest and dependable, then it is more likely that the leader will gain the trust of the team and that the team will reflect the characteristics of the leader. To earn your team's trust, as a leader, you must say what you mean, do what you say, and then lead by example. Leaders know that trust is earned, respect is gained, honesty is appreciated, and loyalty is returned. These statements are often cited as examples of the law of attraction: that you attract what you focus on. For our purposes, we will define trust as "confidence that is proven by consistent, consecutive and coherent action observed." Trust is not faith, which is belief without proof, but actions observed and acknowledged. Trust, therefore, must be earned and cannot be bought or coerced. Lead with the speed of trust and accelerate your team.

> ### Trust
>
> To earn your team's trust as a leader, you must say what you mean, do what you say, and then lead by example. Leaders know that trust is earned, respect is gained, honesty is appreciated, and loyalty is returned.

Leadership is Hope: Napoleon Bonaparte, who ruled France from 1799 to 1815 and led his armies in desperate battles, inspired people to follow him for nearly 20 years. Napoleon famously said: "A leader is a dealer in hope." Napoleon knew that people must believe that the leader will take them through challenges to success. He understood that leaders bring hope from despair. Every team will face challenges. Hope is the belief that events will happen as promised. Hope is a leap of expectation that can fire the imagination of the members of a team to accomplish a goal. Hope is a promise that motivates. False hope is a false promise. Leaders must be truthful and clear-eyed in their promises. Hope starts with visions, not goals, and focuses on the Why and How. A leader instills a hopeful vision of success and explains how this success is achievable, that obstacles can and will be overcome. A leader who can generate hope brings the team through the wilderness, onto a path that everyone can visualize, and ultimately to their desired destination.

> ### Hope
>
> Hope is the belief that events will happen as promised. Hope is a leap of expectation that can fire the imagination of the members of a team to accomplish a goal. Hope is a promise that motivates.

Leadership is Example: The motto of the United States Army Rangers is "Rangers lead the way!" This aphorism acknowledges that all leadership is by example. Leaders must say what they mean and do what they say. Failure to do so will cause a loss of trust and confidence of your team members. According to Albert Schweitzer, 20th-century author, philosopher and polymath, "The three most important ways to lead people are: ... by example... by example... by example." To win, a leader must motivate and impel teammates to act. To do this, leaders must communicate by example and word. Of these two, example is the most powerful. Colorful speeches may be great for the cinema and stirring tweets might rouse some people's emotions, but in the actual world, leaders inspire primarily by example. "Follow me" and subsequently moving forward with your team carries far more influence than "Go ahead, I'm not going, you do it," and staying safely behind. Remember, a leader is always on parade, and every member of your team will be listening to your every word and watching all your actions. The people you lead will instantly know if you if you are leading by example.

Example (action) trumps promise (pledge to do something later) every time. "Setting an example is not the main means of influencing others," scientist, theoretical physicist, philosopher, and genius Albert Einstein said, "it is the only means." All leadership is by example. General George Washington lived this motto during his duties as a leader in war and peace. During the American Revolutionary War, Washington was commander-in-chief of the American military. During the eight years of war against Great Britain, from 1775 to 1783, General Washington never left the Army. He never took a leave away from the Army, but stayed with his men, even in the worst of times, to lead by example. He led from the front, risking his life on countless occasions. Even though many soldiers fell by his side during the battles, Washington never flagged nor failed to lead by example. Although bullets pierced his hat and clothing in several battles, he remained undaunted. Understanding the power of being a role model for the Army and the nation, Washington became the standard for other leaders to emulate. Washington had a genius for leadership. His soldiers were devoted to him, and because of the example he set, they became devoted to the cause of American liberty. There would be no United States of America without George Washington. His leadership was that vital. If you want to know what made George Washington the victor in the long, hard struggle for independence, and later earned him the reputation as the Father of his Country, it can be summed up in four words: He led by example.

Lead by Example

"The three most important ways to lead people are: ... by example...
by example... by example." Albert Schweitzer

Leadership is Influence: Leadership is not authority, position or rank. Leadership is about the ability to influence other human beings. Influence is the power of a person to be a compelling force to produce effects on the actions and character of others. Anyone with desire to encourage and help others can have a positive influence. Influence does not require rank, title, position or power. The most effective leaders in world history had no rank. Jesus Christ and Confucius, who have influenced billions of people over countless generations, had no official position of authority or title. Simon Sinek writes: "Leadership is a choice, not a rank. Anyone in an organization can be a leader... It's choosing to look out for the person on your left and to look out for the person on your right." In his seminal book, *Leadership for the 21st Century* (Praeger, 1993), Joseph C. Rost states that: "Leadership is an influence relationship among leaders and followers who intend real changes that reflect their mutual purposes." Leadership leverages influence, while management imposes authority. The fundamental difference between management and leadership is that leadership requires followers, while management requires subordinates. Leadership, therefore, is a dynamic and reciprocal process of influence between the leader and the team. This same thinking is echoed by John Maxwell when he states: "Leadership is influence, nothing more and nothing less."

Influence

Anyone with the desire to encourage and help others can have
a positive influence. Influence does not require rank, title, position
or power.

Marcus Aurelius stated: "Waste no more time arguing about what a good man should be. Be one." Waste no more time, therefore, arguing what a good leader should be, be one. Start by crafting your own personal definition of leadership to brand your leadership style for all to know. Leaders must communicate.

It is important to the people you lead that you know what leadership is and that you can articulate it to them clearly, simply and succinctly. If you focus on a thoughtfully worded personal definition of leadership, you are apt to improve your ability to understand how to lead. Your definition can help you visualize a sharper image of leadership in your own mind. "Leadership is learned, earned, and discerned," says author and pastor Rick Warren. "You develop it. It's based on trust and credibility. Others see it in you. You can't demand it."

Your Definition of Leadership

Leaders must communicate. It is important to the people you lead that you know what leadership is and that you can articulate it to them clearly, simply, and succinctly... Your definition can help you to visualize a sharper image of leadership in your own mind.

If, as Socrates said, all understanding starts with definition, then your personal definition of leadership can set the standard for how you will lead. As you gain experience, modify and sharpen your definition. Most leaders I have met, in the military, business and government, have never taken the time to construct a personal definition of leadership. You should be the exception. Think about it. What is your personal definition of leadership? Do not copy a definition from someone else. Imagine explaining this definition to those you lead and using it as a rally point to increase leadership awareness among your team members. On the next page, write your personal definition of leadership in 1–5 sentences. Construct it with care, carefully choosing each word. Use both focus and passion in developing your definition. Try to visualize it in your mind and feel it in your heart. Use active voice, first person, so that your personal definition of leadership starts like this: Leadership is....

My Personal Definition of Leadership:

Leadership is_____

_____

_____

_____

_____

_____

_____

_____

_____

_____

_____

_____

_____

_____

_____

_____

_____

_____

_____

_____

You have just taken another critical step on your leadership journey. You cannot truly understand something unless you first state it in your own words. If you can define it, you can visualize it, measure it, and then improve it. As referenced previously, Socrates, the great ancient Greek philosopher, said: "All understanding starts with definition." If you wish to understand leadership, your personal definition of leadership must describe how you want to lead. If someone that you lead were to ask you: "What is leadership?" and you reply "I'm not sure. I never really thought about it," how inspiring is that?

Your definition of leadership provides a personal standard to measure your actions as a leader. A cynical or cryptic definition such as, "A leader is what a leader does," is not very helpful. Create and refine your definition as if you wanted to persuade someone to believe, trust and follow you as if everything depended on this. When your definition is complete, test it. Get someone to play devil's advocate and "Red Team" your definition. Red Teaming involves thinking like the opponent to rigorously challenge ideas, plans, and assumptions. Discuss your personal definition with as many trusted people as possible and let them act as your Red Team. Listen, pause and reflect on their reactions and comments. If you find that in this process of interaction your definition falls short, then adjust it. Vow to continuously review and improve your definition to ensure it is a standard you believe in. Your personal definition of leadership must become an essential part of your personal brand.

I developed my definition of leadership over many years of learning from my parents, in school, sports, my 30 years in the United States Army, in business and in self-study. My personal definition of leadership is: "Leadership is the art of influence and a sacred trust. It is the ability to impel people to work together as a team to accomplish a mission. Leadership requires the unending development of the leader's character, competencies, and commitment to be successful. Leadership is a journey, not a destination."

For me, leadership is clearly the art of influence. To influence, you must inspire, or impel, and avoid resorting to "compel" unless there are no other options and in extreme situations. I believe that leadership is a sacred trust. At a minimum, as a leader, I am responsible for your time, and time is the essence of life. To waste your time is to waste your life. If you are on my team, therefore, I will work mightily not let you down. This is the promise I make with my teammates, and I take it as a point of honor to diligently keep that promise.

In life, we all rise to the level of our leadership. If your leadership level is high, you can make an extraordinary, positive impact. If your leadership level is low, your life will be difficult; you will have a limited ability to work with other people, and a diminished capacity to change things for the better. In any situation involving two or more people, leadership is important. Every leader holds in his or her hands the fate of the people they lead. For the military, police, firefighters and first responders, the role of the leader can literally mean the difference between life or death. In other occupations, the leader controls the hours of work of the people in their team. Hours constitute quality of life, and if squandered by poor leadership, will cause waste, abuse and failure. For this reason, I believe that leadership is a sacred trust, because it involves people. There is no more precious resource on your team than the people you lead.

In any group, leaders make the difference between success or failure, victory or defeat. Effective leadership can produce synergy and create teams that can be more than the sum of their parts. They magnify the people in the team to create a greater leverage than the individuals could have if they worked alone.

Being a leader can be a challenge, but the experience offers intrinsic rewards. Leading a team through hardships and disappointment can test your resilience and commitment. Overcoming setbacks to build and lead a winning team can be an electrifying experience. Learning to lead, and leading well, can be extremely fulfilling. If you consistently raise your leadership awareness through study, and continually seek opportunities to gain leadership experience, your leadership abilities will grow. Ultimately, understanding leadership is essentially a journey about understanding one's self. Self-awareness is the key. There is no greater reward than to unlock your ability to influence, motivate, inspire and lead people effectively to succeed.

In today's competitive, ever-changing and hyperactive world of business, the companies and teams that win are those whose people are most skilled, focused and passionate about accomplishing their mission, be it bringing a new product to market or delivering world-class service. The primary ingredients these successful companies and teams have in common are exceptional leaders; leaders on a lifelong journey to master the skills of influencing people to succeed and make things better than they were before. To update Heraclitus, who I quoted at the start of this chapter: "Out of every 100 people who work for an organization, ten should not even be here, 80 are just path-followers and do the bare minimum, nine are skilled supervisors and managers, and we are lucky to have them, for they keep the organization afloat. Ah, but the one, the one is a true leader, a pathfinder with the character, competency and commitment required to impel everyone to work together and achieve the goal." In the next chapter, we will use this spirit to determine your personal "superpowers."

Chapter Summary

1. There are scores of managers, many supervisors, but few genuine leaders. Extraordinary leaders take the time to develop a personal definition of leadership and then live by that definition.

2. As a pathfinder studies the ravines, hills and rivers of a territory before embarking on a journey; a successful leader reads the human terrain before acting.

3. There is no simple recipe for leadership. Leadership is multifaceted and complex, yet achievable when the character, competencies and commitment of the leader are in harmony. Creating your own personal definition of leadership enhances that harmony.

4. Leaders must communicate. It is important to the people you lead that you know what leadership is and that you can articulate it to them clearly, simply and succinctly. Your definition can help you to visualize a sharper image of leadership in your own mind.

5. If all understanding starts with definition, then your personal definition of leadership can set the standard for how you lead.

6. As you gain experience as a leader, learn from that experience to modify and sharpen your definition.

7. Every leader should have a personal definition of leadership and continue to evolve that definition along their leadership journey. The author's personal definition of leadership is: "Leadership is the art of influence and a sacred trust. It is the ability to impel people to work together as a team to accomplish a mission." Leadership requires the unending development of the leader's character, competencies and commitment to be successful. Leadership is a journey, not a destination.

CHAPTER 5

Develop Your Leadership Superpowers

Unleash Your Potential

The superheroes who appear in many of our popular movies today are the mythological champions of our modern age. In ancient times, storytellers would tell the sagas of courageous and noble humans who became role models of strength, wisdom and virtue. From the story of the ancient Sumerian epic poem of Gilgamesh, the gods, demigods and warriors of Homer's *Iliad*, the foundation story of Rome in Virgil's *Aeneid*, the oral stories of the nine worlds of the Vikings, drawn from a collection of poems known today as the "Poetic Edda," and from similar cultural myths of the ancient world, humans have always reveled in the tales of heroes with extraordinary powers. These characters served as societal archetypes, to emulate or abhor, and they are remarkably similar across all cultures and times. In nearly every story, there is a climactic battle between good and evil, life and death, and light and darkness. These ancient myths were an important part of everyday life and provided entertainment, inspiration and moral lessons to their people. In many cases, they served a secondary purpose; to explain a dangerous and chaotic world and provide meaning to birth, life, struggle, death, and thoughts of an afterlife.

Myths are stories based on culture and tradition. Today, we have reinterpreted ancient myths to create new ones. Our superheroes live in galaxies far, far, away, or are comic book characters, like Thor, which trace their roots back to original Norse myths, but now exist in a modern world. In contemporary movies, these superheroes play much the same role as the characters of ancient myths. They engage in some great struggle, usually a classic battle between good and evil, and along the way, they provide us indirect guidance on how to understand our lives. The best of these films are also very entertaining, which is the measure of any wonderful story. Think about the superheroes you enjoy watching. Most have one or two things they excel at more than anyone else. Some have great strength, like the Hulk, while others are as clever as Odysseus, like Iron Man, or as true and courageous a leader as Captain America.

These modern-day myths, whether they come from comic books or movies, can provide us with a fun way to understand the power of role models. Brodi Ashton, a *New York Times* best-selling author, wrote in her book *Everneath* (Balzer and Bray, 2012): "Heroes are made by the path they choose, not the powers they are graced with." Special powers can assist you along your journey, but the most heroic thing that any of us can do is to choose the right path. The superpowers these characters display are purposefully exaggerated to make a point, but did you know that superpowers really exist? You can develop your own amazing and exceptional powers. The superpowers I am speaking of will not let you run at super speeds like Flash, or empower you to do Jedi mind tricks like Obi-Wan Kenobi, but they may help you to do something even more extraordinary. They can make you a better leader. As Superman once said (in the second title in the *All-Star DC Comics* line): "You are much stronger than you think you are. Trust me." Superman said this to a young woman who was contemplating suicide. He talked her out of it, partly by showing her that she had more courage than she felt she had. He didn't need superpowers to do this. He only had to care enough to get involved. In this story, Superman, the Man of Steel, showed us that our greatest strengths are how we treat other human beings. This is an important leadership lesson.

Heroes

"Heroes are made by the path they choose, not the powers they are graced with."
Brodi Ashton[*]

There are many superpowers that you can develop. The wonderful thing about these superpowers is that everyone has the capability to do so. You do not have to be strong, fast, super-smart, rich, or young to possess any of these. The best news is these superpowers are free to anyone. To develop your own set of superpowers, all you have to do is recognize your inherent talents and nurture them. "You are your own raw material," Warren Bennis, an American scholar, organizational consultant and author, who pioneered the contemporary field of "Leadership Studies," said. "When you know what you consist of and what you want to make of it, then you can invent yourself."

---

[*] This quote is often misattributed to Iron Man, and you will find it on T-Shirts and posters with Iron Man's image, but it comes from Brodi's book *Everneath*.

What are your superpowers? If you develop one, you may be surprised how much it can energize your leadership. Here are a few of the superpowers to consider: humility, gratitude, listening, being a good follower, being a lifelong learner and selflessness.

Superpower #1: Humility

This is probably the greatest superpower that anyone can possess and one of the most difficult to obtain. Superman, possibly the greatest hero in the DC Comics world, is the humblest of all the superheroes. He has god-like powers, but his story is not the thirst for power, but for truth, justice and hope. Superman was the first superhero and his values appealed to pop culture because they are endearing and perennial. Near the ending of the classic *Superman, The Movie* with Christopher Reeve, Superman captures the arch villain of the film, Lex Luthor, and flies him to the penitentiary. As he lands Lex in the prison yard, the warden comes out and says: "This country is safe again, Superman, thanks to you." Superman answers: "No, sir. Don't thank me, Warden. We're all part of the same team. Good night." Humility indeed.

> ### Less "I" and More "We"
>
> The most effective leaders are humble. They get it. They use less "I" and more "We."
> They talk of their team, not themselves. They give credit to others.

You do not have to be Superman to develop humility as your superpower. Humility can become your set of armor, guarding you from negativity. Humility is the quality of being unassuming and having an awareness of your place in the universe. It is an understanding of modesty to know who you are and that you can be happy with your role in the world. You cannot buy humility and you cannot gift it. Humility is about who you are, how you define yourself, and how you act. There is truth in humility, as being truly humble is a realization of your personal worth on your own terms. It is the opposite of humiliation. "Humility leads to strength and not to weakness," said American lawyer, diplomat and presidential advisor John J. McCloy. "It is the highest form of self-respect to admit mistakes and to make amends for them."

Humility matters in leaders and we all need to understand it better. The most effective leaders are humble. They get it. They use less "I" and more "we."

They are modest about their own achievements and talk about the efforts and accomplishments of their team, not themselves. They give credit to others. No leader can do it all as it takes a team to accomplish monumental tasks. Outstanding leaders know the value of people. A skilled leader knows that accomplishment results from many people working together. No one gets anywhere alone. Someone invested in you. Your parents, your relatives, your teachers, your team, all invested in you. You may think you achieved success solely on your own merits, but the world we live in today is the product of many who came before you; they have a hand in your success.

C. S. Lewis, the famous author of the *Chronicles of Narnia,* said:

> Do not imagine that if you meet a really humble man he will be what most people call "humble" nowadays: he will not be a sort of greasy, smarmy person, who is always telling you that, of course, he is nobody. Probably all you will think about him is that he seemed a cheerful, intelligent chap who took a real interest in what you said to him. If you do dislike him it will be because you feel a little envious of anyone who seems to enjoy life so easily. He will not be thinking about humility: he will not be thinking about himself at all. If anyone would like to acquire humility, I can, I think, tell him the first step. The first step is to realize that one is proud. And a biggish step, too. At least, nothing whatever can be done before it. If you think you are not conceited, it means you are very conceited indeed.

Few of us like to be around conceited people. Few of us think that we are conceited. We are, however, all guilty, some more than others. But what C. S. Lewis stated as the first step to learn to be humble is profound: "If you think you are not conceited, you are very conceited indeed." In Rick Warren's successful book, *The Purpose-Driven Life* (Zondervan, 2013), Warren relates this line of thinking this way: "Humility is not thinking less of yourself, it's thinking of yourself less." That is a superpower to embrace if you choose to become an exceptional leader.

Humility rejects the idea that you must compare yourself with others. This kind of comparative analysis occurs when we envy others for what they are or what they have. Envy and jealousy are the negative emotions that arise when you compare yourself with someone else and see yourself as less. People filled with envy and jealousy only torment themselves and these emotions can poison your life. If you let envy and jealousy rule your actions, you will never escape from the trap. There will always be someone with more money, a better home, a fancier car, significant fame, or with greater power than you. Humility shows you that happiness is not from these things. Seeking happiness in things, and comparing yourself with others, are self-inflicted wounds. You damage yourself when you live by comparative analysis. You can avoid this trap by centering yourself and choosing to be humble. Your idealized image of other people's success or happiness is likely an illusion. If it were not so, you would seldom hear about all the successful, rich and powerful people who self-destruct every day. If they have everything, why does this happen? Perhaps they are missing something more important than instant gratification, money and power. If the possession of shiny objects drives you, what will you do once you achieve them? You have a choice and do not have to let these external influences drive you. You have the power, through humility, to be happy with who you are, with what you have, and thus to remove the power of these distractions over you. Doing so will make you a better person, and a better leader.

Humility

Humility rejects the idea that you must compare yourself with others. This kind of comparative analysis occurs when we envy others for what they are or what they have. Envy and jealousy are the negative emotions that arise when you compare yourself with someone else and see yourself as less. These emotions can poison your life.

Humility is a choice and a secret to success. It is a vital attribute of exceptional leaders, and a superpower you can develop. Humility does not mean a lack of ambition. You can be humble and ambitious. Ambition by itself is common. Ambition plus intellectual humility is a powerful combination. Humble ambition is the goal. The next time you are feeling conceited, check your attitude. Change your perspective. An example of how to build humility is to be aware of whom you give the credit to for accomplishing goals. Are you the one who shines and hogs the spotlight, or do you reflect any successes to your team members who did the work? Successful leaders praise the meritorious and commend the team for every success. They do this out of a genuine feeling in their heart, not because it looks good.

Rick Pitino, a successful American basketball coach and the head coach of Panathinaikos of the Greek Basket League (the first-tier basketball league in Greece) and the EuroLeague, said: "Humility is the true key to success. Successful people lose their way at times. They often embrace and overindulge from the fruits of success. Humility halts this arrogance and self-indulging trap. Humble people share the credit and wealth, remaining focused and hungry to continue the journey of success." Develop an attitude of humble ambition to do something for the greater good. There can be no leadership without ambition but focus your ambition on the team's goals rather than proudly serving yourself. Target selflessness as your goal. "Humility," Simon Sinek reminds us, "must never be confused with meekness. Humility is being open to the ideas of others." Keep the commitment and drive, but share the credit, and aim to raise everyone on the team to a higher level. Even better than sharing the credit, give all the credit to those who deserve it. Anything less is conceit. In short, do not shine, reflect.

> ### Shine or Reflect?
>
> **Successful leaders praise the meritorious and commend the team for every success.**
> **Leaders do not shine, they reflect.**

Superpower #2: Gratitude

Another wonderful superpower that anyone can possess is an attitude of gratitude. Gratitude is the quality of being thankful and a readiness to show appreciation for, and to return, kindness. Developing a sense of gratitude rewires your brain to make you more positive, improves your mental health, your ability to sleep, and improves your self-esteem. "Gratitude is the healthiest of all human emotions," said leadership expert Zig Ziglar. "The more you express gratitude for what you have, the more likely you will have even more to express gratitude for." Germany Kent, an American award-winning journalist, businesswoman, and best-selling author, said this about gratitude: "It's a funny thing about life, once you begin to take note of the things you are grateful for, you begin to lose sight of the things that you lack." All it takes to realize gratitude is to comprehend the tremendous gift we have given for being alive and for the opportunity to make a difference. Doris Day, an American acting and singing megastar of the 1960s, and an animal welfare activist, said it best: "Gratitude is riches. Complaint is poverty."

Think of all the things in life you take for granted. Imagine that you were swimming in a lake on a beautiful summer day. Suddenly, without warning, a powerful swirling vortex pulls you down. You struggle to swim upward, but the circling waters entrap you. You are pulled underwater and your air is running out. How grateful would you be to break free, rise to the surface and breathe in a gulp of fresh air? How much would that mouthful of air be worth to you? Everything! How often do we all take the simple act of breathing for granted? Gratitude is about seeing the bigger picture and realizing the true value of everything around you. There is an anonymous saying that expresses great wisdom about gratitude: "It is not happy people who are thankful. It is thankful people who are happy." Gratitude can become your amazing superpower on your leadership journey.

> ### An Attitude of Gratitude
>
> Developing a sense of gratitude rewires your brain to make you more positive, improves your mental health, your ability to sleep, and improves your self-esteem... "It is not happy people who are thankful. It is thankful people who are happy."

There is a science behind being grateful. Robert A. Emmons, a leader in the study of positive psychology and a professor at the University of California-Davis, has studied and written about the power of being grateful. Emmons "discovered that gratitude is a deeper, more complex phenomenon that plays a critical role in human happiness. Gratitude is literally one of the few things that can measurably change people's lives." Emmons, who also published the book *Thanks! How the New Science of Gratitude Can Make You Happier* (Mariner Books, 2008), discovered during a 10-week study that people who had an attitude of gratitude were 25 percent happier than those who were ungrateful. He asked grateful people to keep a gratitude journal and list all the things that were going right in their lives that day. The difference was dramatic. All the test subjects did was to list their blessings instead of brooding on things that were going wrong. By switching their brains to gratitude, they changed their attitude. You cannot be grateful and anxious at the same time. Focus on the positive and you can cancel out the negative. You cannot think negatively and be a positive person. The famous American poet, Maya Angelou, expressed her thoughts about gratitude in this elegant, positive way: "This a wonderful day. I've never seen this one before."

By definition, ungrateful people are resentful and, therefore, unhappy. They feel that they are victims of someone or some system because of some real or perceived injustice. They use comparative analysis and contrast their lives with others, or idealized illusions of others, as seen in the media. Resentful people are more likely to be more prone to acts of violence against other people. Resentment is another poison that you must detoxify from your life. Feelings of resentment and unhappiness are self-inflicted. No one can make you happy or unhappy. Only you can do that. Even in your most trying times, to find something to be grateful for can help you overcome the crucible. Make thankfulness a habit. Practice being grateful today, train your attitude of gratitude to become stronger through daily practice. Keep a journal and record each day all that you have to be thankful for. Express gratitude for kindnesses, and when you have a stressful, challenging situation, you will be stronger and more able to adapt, improvise and overcome. Choose an attitude of gratitude.

Gratitude and Happiness

**Feelings of resentment and unhappiness are self-inflicted.
No one can make you happy or unhappy. Only you can do that.**

Superpower #3: An Understanding Heart

Empathy is to have an understanding heart and to share the feelings of another. It is the ability to put yourself in someone else's shoes and truly understand their feelings and emotions. It is not sympathy, which is feeling sorry for someone else. It is not being soft. The United States Army, not an organization many consider to be very empathetic, stresses in its leadership training that leaders must have empathy for their soldiers. The Army field manual on leadership development, FM 6-22, challenges leaders:

> "Do you show empathy? Do you consider the situations of others relating to their challenges?" Empathy is defined as the ability to share and understand someone else's feelings. The capacity for empathy is an important attribute for leaders to possess. Empathy can allow leaders to understand how their actions will make others feel and react. Empathy can help leaders to understand those that they deal with including other soldiers, Army civilians, local populace, and even enemy forces. Being able to see from another's viewpoint enables a leader to understand those around them better.

Being intelligent does not guarantee that you will be empathetic. In fact, the former and the latter are independent. Some very intelligent people lack empathy. Without empathy, just like a plant without water, the relationship between the leader and the team will wither and die. A leader with a balanced sense of empathy can sense and understand the human condition on both an individual and a group level. Empathy is about understanding human beings and what drives them and can help create successful relationships, reduce anxiety, and raise emotional intelligence. William James, a 19th-century American philosopher and psychologist, known as the "Father of American psychology," said: "The deepest craving of human nature is the need to be appreciated." This is a profound statement and is the heart of having empathy for other people. You must appreciate the people you lead.

In his book on empathy, Daniel Goleman, the internationally known psychologist and author of the best-selling book *Emotional Intelligence Why It Can Matter More Than IQ* (Bantam, 2005), defines three kinds of empathy: cognitive, emotional, and compassionate. Cognitive empathy is intellectual understanding and is as much about thoughts as about emotions. Goleman defines this as "simply knowing how the other person feels and what they might be thinking. Sometimes called perspective-taking, this kind of empathy can help in, say, a negotiation or in motivating people." The downside of cognitive empathy is that the leader may seem cold and unemotional without really having a true sense of sympathy. Emotional empathy is when you genuinely recognize how someone feels and you begin to mirror that emotion. This "emotional contagion" can have negative effects on a leader and a team, to the point of paralysis. Leaders benefit from empathy but cannot allow emotional contagion. Compassionate empathy, according to Goleman, helps leaders to understand the other person's feelings, and share those feelings, but the leader remains capable of acting to help that person or change the situation for the better.

In short, cognitive empathy is intellectual (mind only and less emotional); emotional empathy is all feelings (heart only and over-emotional); and compassionate empathy is the convergence of mind and heart (balanced) to mitigate the problem. Goleman believes that leaders benefit by understanding all three types of empathy and learning how to develop and exhibit emotional intelligence. Emotional intelligence is the ability to understand and influence the emotions of yourself, of others, and of groups. To use a Star Trek analogy, do not act like Commander Spock (logical—cognitive empathy) when you need to be Doctor McCoy (emotional empathy), and do not mimic McCoy when you need to be Captain Kirk (compassionate empathy with a bias for action). Develop and employ all three by exercising your emotional intelligence.

Star Trek and Empathy

To use a Star Trek analogy, do not act like Commander Spock (logical–cognitive empathy) when you need to be Doctor McCoy (emotional empathy), and do not mimic McCoy when you need to be Captain Kirk (compassionate empathy with a bias for action).

So how can you improve your emotional intelligence as a leader? First, you must be in command of your own emotions and be self-aware. Know your own emotions. "If your emotional abilities aren't in hand," Goleman explains, "if you don't have self-awareness, if you are not able to manage your distressing emotions, if you can't have empathy and have effective relationships, then no matter how smart you are, you are not going to get very far." You react with emotion to certain events to help you survive. Emotion is feedback, and something you should pay attention to. Becoming over-emotional, losing control of yourself, is something leaders must avoid. Learn what triggers you to fear or rage; knowing this is the challenge. Control your impulsive thoughts and exchange the negative movie playing in your head with a positive one. You control the "cinema of your mind." You must learn to command your own emotions and motivate yourself before you can hope to lead others.

Second, learn to upgrade your emotional awareness of others. Do they appear happy, sad, mad, anxious, confused, scared, tired, or overwhelmed? Recognizing and understanding other people's emotions is a valuable human skill. Sincerely reacting to the emotions, you identify in others a pathway for you to connect with them. Alfred Adler, an Austrian doctor and psychotherapist (1870–1937) said it best: "Empathy is seeing with the eyes of another, listening with the ears of another, and feeling with the heart of another."

Third, learn to manage relationships and influence the emotions of others. If you can tune into the emotional frequency of your team, you can motivate and inspire them to action. Accomplish this by leading by example, planning, deciding, communicating, persuading, and building collaboration. You create a synergistic teamwork environment through training, teaching and coaching both your individual employees and your collective team.

Controlled Breathing to Reduce Stress

When you are excited or fearful, learn to center yourself and control your breathing using the "4-7-8" breathing method. Breathe in quietly through your nose for four seconds then hold the breath for a count of seven seconds, then exhale forcefully through the mouth, rounding your lips, for eight seconds.

One way to stay centered and avoid emotional contagion is to understand the role of breathing. Most of us take breathing for granted but learning to control your breathing is a powerful skill. When you are excited or fearful, learn to center yourself and control your breathing by using the "4-7-8" breathing method. Breathe in quietly through your nose for four seconds, then hold the breath for a count of seven seconds, then exhale forcefully through the mouth, rounding your lips, for eight seconds. Do this several times and you will find that you become more relaxed. Several repetitions of deep breathing in this manner can calm and regulate the autonomic nervous system. In the military, this is called tactical breathing and it works. This simple method can help you in times of stress.

Developing empathy and using it to understand people can make you a more effective leader. Using empathy as emotional radar is indispensable. If you look at emotion as a method of communication, it can be positive or negative, effective or ineffective. Use your empathy radar to gauge the mood of your individuals and the team, but do not become infected with "emotional contagion." Emotional contagion is a situation where another person's emotions and related behaviors directly trigger similar emotions in other people. It is the "sympathetic detonation" of unanticipated behaviors that can quickly run rampant through a team. This can be helpful if a positive outcome is to rally the team on an emotional level, but it can just as easily cloud the leader's judgment and disrupt his or her decision-making. You must consider the difference between understanding, and not mirroring, your team members' feelings when empathy is appropriate for the situation. Panic is an emotion that has powerful, sympathetic emotional detonation in groups and has destroyed armies, companies and teams. Exceptional leaders turn situations of panic into patience, purpose and courage. When the Avengers were at their lowest point in the movie *Avengers: End Game*, Captain America turned their despair into courage by reminding them: "This is the fight of our lives, and we're going to win. Whatever it takes." Captain America's superpower is his principled leadership. In that moment, his understanding and employment of empathy helped him inspire his team to summon their last ounce of courage to rally and win the day.

Superpower #4: Listening

Do not just hear; listen. Listening is a skill most of us need to improve, so why not make it your superpower? How extraordinary would it be if you were renowned as a good listener? What if you were the best listener in your company, group, or team? Active listening is a skill you can learn. Being in the moment, listening intently, and not allowing anything to distract you from listening to the person who is communicating with you, is the greatest honor you can bestow upon another person. "When people talk, listen completely," Ernest Hemingway, a brilliant novelist and adventurer of the 20th century, advised: "Most people never listen." Imagine if you were not like most people and truly listened?

Listening requires focus. Clear your mind of your personal thoughts and focus solely on the person you wish to listen to. Give the speaker the courtesy of your full attention. Develop an attitude of directed, disciplined and active thinking. "Directed" means that your complete focus is on the person communicating with you. "Disciplined" infers that you eliminate or disregard all distractions and prioritize the speaker's message. "Active thinking" involves the sustained mental state required to understand, visualize and reflect on the other person's ideas, with the intent of providing informed feedback. John Maxwell, leadership author and mentor, put it this way: "Leaders should have less direction, more connection. How? Through asking questions and by listening. Here's what I also know, the leader who doesn't listen soon will have people around him or her who have nothing to say. If your people are silent, it's because you don't listen." If your people are quiet, it is because you are talking more than listening. Asking informed questions and fully understanding the answers is an art. Learn to ask the right questions.

Listen Completely

"When people talk, listen completely. Most people never listen."
Ernest Hemingway

The military understands the vital necessity for leaders to communicate effectively and instructs leaders in the art of public speaking in both practice and study. The U.S. Army's manual on leadership, *Army Leadership and the Profession* (ADP 6-22, published in 2019), expresses the obligation for leaders to engage in active listening (by listening and watching attentively, taking appropriate notes, and using verbal and nonverbal means to show the person you are paying attention to them); speaking to create a shared understanding (by expressing thoughts and ideas clearly, keeping key players informed, and sharing necessary information); and making use of engaging communication techniques (such as projecting confidence, maintaining eye contact, using appropriate gestures, and speaking in a manner to engage the listener); and to be sensitive to cultural and personal factors (demonstrate respect for others). The manual states: "Communication is essential to all other leadership competencies."

Active listening builds trust and rapport. People want you to hear them, and active listeners address this need by paying full attention to the speaker. In any conversation, in-person or otherwise, the listener should summarize the speaker's central points at the end of the session and the listener must be willing to adjust his or her summary if the speaker believes a particular part is incorrect. Focus on the person speaking, rather than on your thoughts and answers. "Most people do not listen with the intent to understand;" Stephen Covey explains, "they listen with the intent to reply." Active listening shares understanding by directing the listener's focus outward from self, providing the listener with the opportunity to learn a new perspective. Active listeners do not interrupt. Here is a simple equation that may help improve your listening superpower: Listen + Pause + Understand + Pause + Reflect + Pause + Provide Feedback. The pauses are crucial. If you rush to answer someone, or attempt to complete their sentences for them, you are not listening; you are focused on your own thoughts and planning an answer before hearing the other person out. M. Scott Peck, an American psychiatrist and best-selling author of the book *The Road Less Traveled, A New Psychology of Love, Traditional Values, and Spirit* (Touchstone, 1980), said: "You cannot truly listen to anyone and do anything else at the same time." Practice these methods, focus on the speaker, and make active listening one of your superpowers.

> ## Active Listeners Do Not Interrupt
>
> A simple equation to improve your listening superpower:
> Listen + Pause + Understand + Pause + Reflect + Pause + Feedback =
> Active Listening

Superpower #5: Being a Good Follower

To be an effective leader, you must first be a good follower. This may sound counterintuitive, but it is not. The best leaders are also great followers. All of us follow someone. Being a good follower involves giving up some of your own desires and ego for the good of the team. Leadership is not about shouting orders and always being in charge. Leadership requires discipline, dedication and obedience. All teams require some obedience. Good followers are in high demand. If you want to increase your influence on any team, be the best follower on the team. If you want to learn how to lead, start by being a good follower, and support the team leader. To be a good follower, you must subordinate yourself to something greater than yourself. If you act selflessly and put the team first, others will recognize your efforts and are more likely to follow you.

Learning to follow can develop influence. When you exhibit a positive and supportive attitude, you are practicing leadership as you are setting an example for others to follow. You may not have the title or authority, but if you do the work in a way that inspires others, you are leading within your team. All leadership is by example, and when you set the example, you influence those around you to do the same. Author John S. McCallum, writing in the *Ivey Business Journal* in 2013, stated that followership is the flipside of leadership.

> Followership is a straightforward concept. It is the ability to take direction well, to get in line behind a program, to be part of a team and to deliver on what is expected of you. It gets a bit of a bad rap! How well the followers follow is probably just as important to enterprise success as how well the leaders lead… Quite simply, where followership is a failure, not much gets done and/or what does get done is not what was supposed to get done.

Put another way: What kind of person do you want on your team? Someone who is selfless, punctual, trustworthy, skilled, dedicated and supportive? If so, be that kind of person and you will take a major step forward in becoming an effective leader.

Leaders Learn to Follow

To be an effective leader, you must first be a good follower.

If being a good follower is training to become an outstanding leader, and if you must learn to obey orders before you are qualified to give them, then the example you set for your team when you are a good follower shows everyone your commitment to the team. The respect, commitment and enthusiasm you display in obeying the instructions of your leaders will reflect upon you. Being an unwilling follower or rebelling against your leader only leads to disruption, disrespect, and hinders the team from accomplishing its assigned tasks. Good followers can act in ways that influence their leaders to help them make better decisions and assist them in achieving the organization's goals. This does not mean blind, unprincipled obedience to unscrupulous orders. If you have your principles in sight, if you follow the values of your internal compass, if you align your character, competencies and commitment with your team's goals, then you will act with virtue and be a good follower. Exemplary leaders, therefore, are by definition exemplary followers. Make this one of your superpowers.

Superpower #6: Lifelong Learning

How many books do you read each year? According to author and "brain coach" Jim Kwik, successful CEOs and executives read four to five books *every week*. These leaders know that knowledge is power. Leaders read to ignite their creativity, empower motivation, and unlock their potential. The greatest leaders throughout history have been relentless in their pursuit of knowledge. *Ancora imparo* is an Italian phrase meaning "Yet, I am learning." There is a beautiful, and likely apocryphal story, that the Renaissance polymath Michelangelo said this phrase when someone asked him why he was studying. Michelangelo was 87 at the time and was passionate to learn as long as he breathed. Whether the story is true or not, it fits Michelangelo, a man born in Florence, Italy, in 1475, who made lifelong learning his superpower. Michelangelo created paintings, music, sculpture, architecture, poetry and works of military engineering during his long life. He carved *The Pieta* from marble, making the cold stone come alive, when he was only 23. Later, with hammer and chisel, he created *The David* and he painted the mural on the ceiling of the Sistine Chapel. Sculpting in stone is hard and dangerous work. He never wore eye protection for he said that he had to see the colors of the stone. When he rested from this strenuous work he often jotted down poetry. He studied anatomy to become an expert on the human form. His works remain some of the most famous and adored in history. He was still working on a sculpture, the *Rondanini Pieta,* when he died. *Ancora imparo* indeed!

Becoming a lifelong learner means that you are teachable. You learn from experience and seek knowledge, not to be a know-it-all, but to be a learn-it-all, with the intent of applying that knowledge for some greater good. If you generate the motivation to learn every day and focus that learning on something you are passionate about, you can turn learning into mastery. In every field, reading can be your key to unlock the treasure chest of learning. You can improve your personal and professional knowledge through self-teaching. Educate yourself and read to lead. Read on a daily basis, even if it is only a single page. If you read for 45 minutes a day, at an average reading rate, you will be able to complete four to five books per month. Reading is active learning and requires your brain to visualize what you read, creating an image in your head that can last longer than a picture or video you passively observe. This is why reading a story from a book "sticks with you" longer than just watching a movie. It is why most people say "I saw the movie. The book was better." Reading is active, while watching a video is passive. You may daydream as you watch a show on television, but you cannot daydream and read at the same time. You either read or daydream. This is why reading is so powerful as it demands focus and concentration. How much knowledge might you add by reading 60 books a year?

Be a Lifelong Learner

Becoming a lifelong learner means that you are teachable. You learn from experience and seek knowledge, not to be a know-it-all, but to be a learn-it-all, with the intent of applying that knowledge for some greater good.

Reading is not your only resource in developing the superpower of lifelong learning. If you want to learn a new skill, take an on-line learning course, or find an in-classroom course at your local community college. Find someone who is an expert at the skill you wish to learn and ask them to teach you. If you believe you have nothing left to learn, think again. You must never stop learning, questioning, and growing your mind. Take every opportunity to learn skills and concepts in your area of expertise. Explore new venues you may never have experienced before. Lifelong learners are not afraid to try and never too embarrassed to say that they are still learning. The more immersive, interactive and memorable the learning, the more deeply you will understand and retain the information. Turn the power of knowledge into your superpower by becoming a lifelong learner.

Superpower #7: Selflessness

Selfless leaders care more about the team and the people they lead than their own personal advancement or glorification. We admire selflessness and dislike selfishness. This tendency has been bred into humanity over millennia as we formed teams to survive and thrive. Selfish people, who did not share with the tribe, were usually excluded from the group. Teamwork, therefore, is a human quality that has evolved with humanity. Teamwork requires a degree of selflessness from everyone in the group, but especially from the leader. "My research debunks the myth that many people seem to have that you become a leader by fighting your way to the top," writes author William Cohen in *The Stuff of Heroes: The Eight Universal Laws of Leadership*. "Rather, you become a leader by helping others to the top. Helping your employees is as important as, and many times more so than, trying to get the most work out of them."

Selflessness

If you are a selfless leader, who puts the benefit of your team members above yourself, you enhance your ability to inspire everyone to do more than just the bare minimum.

If selflessness is intrinsic to teamwork, and teams are necessary to succeed, why are there so many selfish leaders? We have all seen leaders who put themselves and their self-interests above those of the group. In time, however, all selfish leaders fail. Some may maintain the perception of success, and still cling to power or fame, but fail at life. Selfish leadership is self-defeating. The reason selfishness eventually fails is that leading is never about one person. You may think the team exists for your personal benefit, but you cannot lead people solely for your own personal gain for very long. Such leadership is built upon a lie. Eventually, the members of the team see your selfishness and reject your leadership. If they are working for a salary, they may do the minimum, but will not go beyond the letter of their contract. If the leader has coercive power over them, as in a dictatorship, they may obey out of fear, but they will not obey willingly. If you are a selfless leader, who puts the benefit of the team members above yourself, you enhance your ability to inspire everyone to do more than their bare minimum.

"If leadership serves only the leader, it will fail," says Sheila Murray Bethel in *Making a Difference: 12 Qualities That Make You a Leader* (Berkeley Publishing Corporation, 1990). "Ego satisfaction, financial gain, and status can all be valuable tools for a leader, but if they become the only motivations, they will eventually destroy a leader. Service before self. Only when service for a common good is the primary purpose are you truly leading." For selfless leaders, people have moved mountains, explored the unknown, and achieved magnificent accomplishments.

Leadership requires selflessness, the antithesis of selfishness. Selflessness puts the team's well-being ahead of the leader's self-promotion, luxury and comfort. Absolute selflessness is seen in those who pay the last full measure of devotion protecting or saving others, who are lionized as heroes. All exceptional leaders place the well-being of their teammates above their own. We admire the heroic nature of their selflessness and expect this from our leaders. When we are led by someone who is totally selfish, we resent them. The leader serves the team, not the other way around. Selflessness, therefore, is a superpower you can exhibit. To own it, you have to sacrifice on behalf of those you lead. This is one of the reasons effective leadership is so challenging, and also why it is rare. Make selflessness your superpower.

Learning and Developing Your Leadership Strengths

Superpowers are within you and are yours for the taking. There are many other superpowers you might embrace and develop. Some additional superpower suggestions are to speak and write with conviction, to make timely and informed decisions, and the master ability to prepare and execute detailed plans. Knowing your superpowers requires that you first recognize, then understand, your best talents and develop them. These superpowers radiate an inner light that you can possess if you are willing to apply the discipline required to earn them and turn them into habits. In his best-selling self-improvement book, *Atomic Habits*, James Clear states: "Decide the type of person you want to be. Prove it to yourself with small wins." You know what you are best at. You know what you want to be better at. Make these your superpowers. Take small steps every day to improve these skills, and they will help propel you along your leadership path. In our next chapter, we will investigate the central power of leadership: how to decide.

Chapter Summary

1. Modern-day myths, whether they come from comic books or movies, can provide us with a fun way to understand the power of role models.

2. Iron Man said: "Heroes are made by the path they choose, not the powers they are graced with." He knew that his special powers assisted him along his journey, but that the most heroic thing that any of us can do is to choose the right path.

3. You do not have to be strong, fast, super-smart, rich, or young to possess a superpower. Everyone can develop his or her own set of superpowers, and all you have to do is know your inherent talents and nurture them.

4. A few examples of superpowers that you can develop are:
   • Humility: Humility is the quality of being unassuming and having an awareness of your place in the universe.
   • Gratitude: Gratitude is the quality of being thankful and a readiness to show appreciation for, and to return, kindness.
   • An Understanding Heart: Empathy is to have an understanding heart and to share the feelings of another.
   • Listening: Do not just hear, listen.
   • Be a Good Follower: To be an effective leader, you must first be a good follower.
   • Be a Lifelong Learner: Leaders never stop learning and read to ignite their creativity, empower motivation and unlock their potential.
   • Selflessness: Selfless leaders care more about the team and the people they lead than their own personal advancement or glorification.

5. Knowing your superpowers requires that you first recognize, then understand, your best talents and develop them. Superpowers are within you. To energize your expertise is to decide, focus and apply discipline to turn the superpower you want into a habit.

6. Superpowers are within you and are yours for the taking. There are many other superpowers you might embrace and develop.

7. You know what you are best at. You know what you want to be better at. Make these your superpowers. Take small steps every day to improve these skills, and they will help propel you along your leadership path.

NOTES

CHAPTER 6

Shape Your Destiny by Learning How to Decide

Leaders Must Make Plans and Decide

A hard rain struck the roof and windows of Suffolk House like a gale in a tempest. The air was damp and thick with anticipation. The primary decision-makers sat at a long table in the well-furnished manor that acted as the temporary headquarters of the Supreme Headquarters Allied Expeditionary Force (SHAEF). Most of the generals were in a dark mood. The Allied plan was complex, detailed and sophisticated. The group had labored for more than a year for this day and now the horrible weather promised to ruin the plan. The man seated at the head of the table took a deep drag from a cigarette. He was smoking too much these days and getting little sleep. He was 53, but most people felt he looked much older. He did not have time to think about himself now. His focus was the weather.

The looming decision that involved the assembled group was the timing of the greatest amphibious invasion in history. The weather in May had been beautiful with clear skies over most of the French coast, but the forces were not ready. The weather in June had turned miserable. It had rained every day. He had postponed the invasion once already. Initially planned for June 5, the weather forecast issued on June 4 was so terrible that every member of the senior staff agreed to delay the invasion for 24 hours in the hope of better weather. The weather prediction for June 5 turned out to be accurate, with nearly impossible weather. The seas were so rough that many of the Allied ships had to seek safe harbors for fear of being swamped. Timing in war is everything, and everything was coming down to this moment and one leader's decision.

General Dwight David Eisenhower, the Supreme Allied Commander, took another puff from a half-burned cigarette and then smashed it out in an ashtray, as if he was crushing out a dark thought. He had assembled his commanders to hear the latest weather reports. His decision would determine the fate of thousands of soldiers and, most likely, the outcome of the war. Several of the senior generals at the table wondered if Eisenhower would measure up to the task. The previous day, Eisenhower had briefed the leader of the Free French Forces in exile, General Charles De Gaulle. The dour Frenchman lectured him for an hour about the errors, miscalculations, and folly of Eisenhower's ill-conceived invasion plan. Eisenhower listened patiently but he put De Gaulle's objections and all doubts aside. His mission was succinct and clear: "You will enter the continent of Europe and, in conjunction with the other united nations, undertake operations aimed at the heart of Germany and the destruction of her armed forces."

Up to the Task

His decision would decide the fate of thousands of soldiers and, most likely, the outcome of the war. Several of the senior generals at the table wondered if Eisenhower would measure up to the task.

To himself, he wondered what words he would use if the invasion failed. He prepared a brief note: "Our landings in the Cherbourg-Havre area have failed to gain a satisfactory foothold, and I have withdrawn the troops. My decision to attack at this time and place was based on the best information available. The troops, the air and the Navy did all that bravery and devotion to duty could do. If any blame or fault attaches to the attempt, it is mine alone."

The time was 4 a.m., Monday, June 5, 1944. If the invasion was to take place on June 6, Eisenhower had to decide in the next few minutes. The clock was ticking. His chief meteorologist, Group Captain James M. Stagg, stood in front of the table, prepared to brief. Eisenhower nodded for him to begin. A slight smile crossed Stagg's lips. "I think we have found a gleam of hope for you, sir." Stagg's briefing lasted for 15 minutes. When it concluded, Eisenhower paused, and then responded, "So, what you are telling me, Stagg, is that we may have a brief period of barely tolerable weather."

"Yes sir," Captain Stagg replied in his Scottish brogue, looking down at the latest weather report in his hand. "Atmospheric surface pressure is rising steadily. This indicates a forecast of a window of marginal weather for the Normandy Coast for at least 18 hours, possibly as long as 24 hours, on June 6th. Wind swells in the Channel at five to six feet, decreasing to three to four feet with three to four-foot wind waves near the invasion beaches. The weather on June 7th remains uncertain."

"How firm is your forecast?" British General Bernard Montgomery, the commander of all Allied ground forces, asked.

"Very firm, sir," Stagg replied, "but not all the SHAEF meteorologists agree with me."

"And the waves will permit us to get the landing craft ashore?" General Omar Bradley, the commander of U.S. First Army, the American ground forces for the invasion, asked.

"The morning will be fair," Stagg said. "Good weather may last through the afternoon."

"Only 18 hours?" Eisenhower questioned.

"Yes sir. I can predict 18 hours of marginal weather from midnight on the 5th of June to the evening of the 6th of June with accuracy," Stagg answered. "Twenty-four hours if we are lucky, but no more than 18 hours."

"Marginal weather?" Air Chief Marshal Arthur Tedder, commander of the Allied air forces, interjected. "Eighteen hours?"

"It's the best forecast I can offer," Stagg replied nervously. "There is a brief improvement in the conditions. The storm front is moving faster than we originally expected. The tide and wave swells are within margin, but cloud coverage could impede bombers from seeing their targets."

"If you decide to go on Tuesday, June 6, we will have to give the order to the Omaha and Utah beach forces in the next half hour," Admiral Bertram Ramsay added. Ramsay, the commander of Allied naval forces, had to plan the movement of the over 5,000 vessels involved in the invasion ranging from naval combatants, landing craft and ships, and naval auxiliaries, to merchant craft. He understood the time-and-space factors involved in maneuvering such a large and diverse naval force. "As you know, the Americans have the farthest to go."

Eisenhower knew that Ramsay was right. The specific planning requirements for the invasion at Normandy offered only 10 days a month for a successful amphibious landing. The Germans knew the invasion was imminent, although they did not know the exact time and location. General Erwin Rommel, one of Germany's finest generals and the man in charge of the German defenses in Normandy, had been improving the defenses of the Atlantic Wall all along the coast of continental Europe and Scandinavia. Rommel had increased the construction of German fortifications and ordered thousands of cleverly designed anti-invasion obstacles sown on every available landing beach.

Rommel had guessed that the Allies would land at high tide and had rigged thousands of beach obstacles with deadly Teller mines. These devices were antitank mines, but they also served as excellent anti-landing craft mines. Each Teller mine contained 11 pounds of explosives. At high tide, the boats would not see the submerged obstacles and, if they hit a mine, it would blow the landing craft out of the water. Many of these Teller mines also had anti-handling devices that would explode the device if Allied engineers tried to disarm them. Eisenhower's planners learned about the beach obstacles and determined that they had to be mitigated. They planned for the landings at low tide, to permit Allied landing craft commanders the ability to identify and circumvent these deadly beach obstacles.

"We have nearly a quarter of a million men on ships, landing craft, airfields and naval embarkation points," Lieutenant General Walter Bedell Smith, Eisenhower's Chief of Staff offered. "We can't keep them waiting indefinitely. And the longer we wait, the more likely the Germans will discover our plan. The next time the moon and tide will be right will be on the 19th of June."

Eisenhower knew the fate of the invasion was his decision. He knew that he would have to roll the dice, make his play, and if he chose wrongly, thousands would die. A bloody failure of the invasion of France could extend the war for years. By then, who knows what evil, new weapons the Nazis might create. There were already intelligence reports of a new, long-range missile program, dubbed *Vergeltungswaffen* or Vengeance Weapons by the Germans. There were also credible reports that Nazi scientists were developing a new kind of bomb, more powerful than anything the world had ever seen. If the invasion failed and the Germans had time to marry their missile program with a new powerful means of destruction, the war might last for decades, or worse, end in defeat for the Allies.

Optimism and Pessimism are Infectious

Both optimism and pessimism are infectious. Ike believed that rumors and panic spread more rapidly from the higher echelons of command downward than in any other direction.

Everyone at the table looked at Eisenhower. The clock ticked. The group waited for a decision.

Eisenhower, known by his nickname "Ike," put on his best poker face.

Ike understood that both optimism and pessimism are infectious. He believed that both emotions spread more rapidly from the higher echelons of command downward than in any other direction. If he was too optimistic or too pessimistic, he might influence his commanders. To balance their feelings, he wanted to listen to their personal assessments and their judgments and harmonize a solution that all would accept.

"Sir, I can speak for the airborne forces," Air Commander Trafford Leigh-Mallory, the commander responsible for transporting the British and American paratroopers for Operation *Overlord*, announced. "In this weather, we can expect heavy casualties."

"How heavy?" Ike asked.

"I estimate our losses could be as high as 70 percent in the 101st and 82nd Airborne Divisions," Leigh-Mallory said without flinching.

Several of the officers sitting at the table sat back in their chairs. Air Marshall Tedder shook his head and looked down at the table as if seeing the dead bodies of the young men laid out in front of him. The plan called for the landing of over 13,000 paratroopers, most of them behind Utah Beach. Seventy percent casualties meant the deaths, incapacitation, or capture of at least 9,100 of the Allies' best soldiers.

Ike listened intently, considered the faces of the six prestigious leaders seated at the table, but knew he had little choice, 70 percent casualties or not.

"Well, then I guess it is all up to our trust in Captain Stagg's weather report?" Admiral Ramsay proclaimed. "I've seen these Channel storms change in the blink of an eye. If the swell is too much, our landing craft could capsize. Can we really bet the entire invasion on this weather report?"

"Maybe you should cancel the para-drops," Tedder offered. The room became silent. For an interminable moment, no one spoke.

"Thank you, Stagg. You've done your best," Ike announced, breaking the pause. Stagg nodded and exited the room. The time for discussion was past. Ike rose from his chair. All looked up at him, waiting for his decision. Ike warmed himself at the fire for a moment and then paced the room again in silence.

The silence lasted for five full minutes. The clock ticked. Ike thought about the note he wrote for the press if the invasion failed. He thought about the thousands of brave paratroopers who would jump from C-47 transport planes in the dark and then fight deep inside enemy territory. He thought about the young infantrymen who would storm the beaches into withering German fire. He reweighed every argument for and against in his mind. He did not take counsel of his fears.

"Okay," he said. "Let's go." With those words, General Eisenhower launched the D-Day invasion. On June 6, 1944, in marginal weather, the Allies began the inevitable liberation of Europe from Nazi tyranny. It was one of the most difficult and courageous decisions of World War II. Eisenhower had gathered the finest minds available on his staff to plan and direct the invasion. These were the best leaders and staff experts of their respective disciplines, branches of service, and nations. Their thoughts mattered to Eisenhower, and he listened carefully to each of his advisors, taking stock of their guidance, opinions and fears. He knew, however, that only he could make the final decision. As Supreme Commander, he shouldered the awesome responsibility of the lives of every man and woman in the invasion force. He made sure that everyone knew that he would use every bit of advice and information his commanders and staff could provide him, but once he decided, he owned the decision. Ike took full responsibility. If the invasion failed because the landing craft swamped in rough seas, or the paratroopers were slaughtered, he alone was to blame. He would not castigate the weatherman or anyone else. That was the measure or Eisenhower's leadership.

It would have been understandable if Eisenhower delayed the decision to launch D-Day and waited for perfect weather. Without perfect conditions, the risk increased, but there are never perfect conditions. Making tough decisions with imperfect information is something all of us will face. In business, fortunes are won or lost because CEOs cannot decide in time. Eisenhower had more than fortunes involved in his decision; he had the lives of hundreds of thousands of people and the fate of the free world in his hands. If he had delayed, the next best day predicted was June 19. That date turned out to be the worst gale in a century and would have destroyed the Allies' fleet of small landing craft as much as the Kamikaze winds had destroyed the great Mongol invasion fleet of Japan in 1281. If they postponed the invasion until the next date in July 1944, the Germans would have had more time to prepare and might have discovered the invasion plans. The Germans would have sown more mines on the beaches and placed more anti-invasion obstacles. The Germans would have ample quantities of V-1 rockets to launch at the invasion fleet, and by September, they would have had the newer, more powerful V-2 rockets, ready to blast the invasion ports. If Ike delayed the invasion even longer, the fall weather might postpone the invasion until the early months of 1945. By then, Adolf Hitler might have developed an atomic bomb.

Tough Decisions

Making tough decisions with imperfect information is something all of us will face. In business, fortunes are won or lost because CEOs cannot decide in time.

Eisenhower knew that he would never have foolproof information or perfect weather. He realized the dangers of delay and had to decide based on the best information available. His leadership influenced everyone around him and inspired them to give him their very best efforts. His powers of persuasion were seldom equaled. His steady confidence influenced every member of his team to believe that the invasion would succeed. He always took his job seriously, but never took himself seriously. He did not shine, he reflected, and always gave the credit to others. This inspired people to follow him. His courage impelled others to have courage. During the D-Day planning, passions ran high because the stakes were extreme, and there were many leaders with grave concerns that the weather, or other factors, would wreck the invasion, but Eisenhower's leadership made them all pull together as a team. This is a sterling example of leadership and an excellent case-study in decision-making.

The momentous problem-set that Eisenhower faced just before D-Day is unique, but all leaders face decisions, big and small. Learning from extraordinary cases is an excellent way to improve your ability to decide. Learning how to decide takes practice and how you decide will be the measure of your leadership.

Decision-making is vital to managers, supervisors, and especially, leaders. If a leader is exceptional at motivating, organizing, and inspiring people, but cannot decide, then people will find another leader. Leaders must make good-enough decisions, in time, to solve problems. To make the best decision possible, a leader must understand him- or herself, the opposition, the situation, and comprehend the possible second- and third-order effects. Decisions can be big and small, with either plenty of time to decide or very little. Major decisions are often stressful, enmeshed in bias, complex and uncertain. Avoiding risk is common and being risk averse is often the reason many leaders cannot decide important issues in a timely manner. Decisiveness is the key to effective leadership in any organization.

> ## Decision-Making
>
> The momentous problem-set that Eisenhower faced just before D-Day is unique, but all leaders face decisions, big and small.

Deciding almost always includes uncertainty and risk, because the future is unknown. It is helpful to categorize problems to help leaders navigate the future. Leaders must solve fresh problems every day. Many problems are unique and require original responses from leaders to solve unique problem-sets, but leaders can learn to recognize problems and sort them into three distinct groupings. This can help speed up and improve decision-making. One of my favorite authors concerning decision-making is Professor Keith Grint, Professor of Defense Leadership at Cranfield University, UK, and Deputy Principal (Leadership and Management) at the Defense College of Management and Leadership within the Defense Academy in Shrivenham. Professor Grint has identified three problem sets that he defines as Tame, Critical, and Wicked in his book *Leadership, Management and Command, Rethinking D-Day* (Palgrave Macmillan; 1st edition November 17, 2007) and in his excellent article "Wicked Problems and Clumsy Solutions: the Role of Leadership" (*Clinical Leader*, Vol. 1. No. II, December 2008, BAMM Publications). His experience is vast and studying Grint's works has added invaluable insights to my understanding of leadership and decision-making.

Tame, Critical, and Wicked Problem Sets

We consider tame problems as routine. Grint describes a tame problem as "Known problems with known solutions that are within existing expertise and knowhow. Tame problems are best approached from a management style of leadership, with a structured logical approach." Nearly every business and organization has developed procedural steps to solve these common problems. A linear, follow-the-steps decision-making approach can often deal with a tame problem. Rational compliance to standard operating procedures has proven effective in solving the tame problem in the past, and if the circumstances are similar or exactly as described in procedures, following the steps outlined in the established process usually solves tame problems. Tame problems, therefore, are the realm of managers and supervisors who follow the established guidelines and execute the published, outlined procedures.

Decision-Making Problem Sets

Problem Set	Definition	Solution	Stakeholders
1. Tame	Clear	Process	Manager
2. Critical	Clear, but Time Sensitive	Commander	Experts
3. Wicked	Unique, Complex Time Sensitive No Apparent Solution	Unity of Effort	Many

A critical problem is a crisis and that demands a prompt response, rapid decisions and hands-on leadership. Grint explained a critical problem as one that "causes a crisis and needs immediate action." They fetch uncertainty and fear. "Commanders are needed who will coerce people into action and tell people what to do." A critical problem is a catastrophe, disaster, or accident where a police officer or firefighter arrives, takes charge of the situation, and solves the problem. With a critical problem, people often willingly obey the person who is taking command of the situation as that person is seen as an expert and a leader who is rising to the challenge. If your house was on fire, the leader of the family normally takes charge to get everyone out of the burning building. There are no arguments as the situation is dire. The person who takes charge in the emergency uses authority to solve the problem: "Leave the house, now!" As Grint expresses in his book *Leadership, Management and Command*, it requires a commander, "whose role is to take the required decisive action." The decisive action either resolves the critical problem or requires a change in direction by the leader or commander to address the problem in another way.

A wicked problem is a multidimensional challenge that may have no solution and that has no clear delineation between cause and effect. Wicked problems are often intractable and defy reduction to smaller, solvable problems. Wicked problems cannot be solved with a linear management or critical-command approach. Grint defines wicked problems as "complex problems that hold a multitude of other problems within them."

Unity of Effort

Wicked problems are best addressed by leaders through unity of effort. Unity of effort is the ability to impel others, over whom you have no authority or responsibility, to work with you to achieve a common goal.

We expect leaders to solve problems, but by definition wicked problems are often insurmountable, which is why attempting to solve the issue often spins off a new situation that can have even worse consequences. Wicked problems are often volatile, uncertain, ambiguous and complex social issues. "Sometimes wicked problems have to be accepted and adapted to rather than overcome," Grint explains. "These problems demand leadership that involves everyone, and approaches that look into everything and every possibility." Leaders often have only one opportunity to solve a wicked problem before the problem morphs into something even more daunting. Failure to solve the wicked problem early can often cause the wicked problem to grow and persist. "The leader's role with a Wicked Problem," Grint writes, "is to ask the right questions rather than provide the right answers because the answers may not be self-evident and will require a collaborative process to make any kind of progress." Some wicked problems, such as poverty or crime, or the initial outbreaks of the COVID-19 pandemic, defy most solutions and are only mitigated to a greater or lesser degree. There may be no answer to the wicked problem other than a choice between bad, or worse, outcomes.

Wicked problems are best addressed by leaders through the concept of "unity of effort." Unity of effort is the ability to impel others, over whom you have no authority or responsibility, to work with you to achieve a common goal. Unity of effort requires the highest form of leadership as you do not have the authority to compel others to get the job done, and therefore, is very rare. The goal of unity of effort is to overcome complex problems that defy simple tame or crisis-command solutions by first establishing unity of purpose and then harmonizing a joint response. Author Scott Lawrence defines unity of effort as "the state of harmonizing efforts among multiple organizations working towards a similar objective. This prevents organizations from working at cross purposes and it reduces duplication of effort." Harmonizing is the central action that exemplifies unity of effort. Harmonizing requires a shared vision, mutual trust, and common motivation. Multiple organizations can achieve unity of effort through shared common objectives and vision. Because unity of effort requires a higher order of leadership it is very rare. This is another reason why wicked problems are so complex and seldom solved, as their solution requires a superlative form of leadership: unity of effort.

Categories of Decisions

If decision-making is central to leadership, then how leaders decide, and how we teach decision-making, are crucial to a team's success. There are three broad categories that impact every decision: organizational, informational and operational. The second and third order of effects involving these decisions will frame the success or failure of all organizations.

Organizational decisions decide the "org chart" and designate who and what resources are in each part of the team. If there is confusion over who has the authority and responsibility for getting things done, then the team effort will suffer. Balancing authority and responsibility for mission accomplishment is indispensable to proper organizational structure. If you want a successful software development project to succeed, but you assign no software engineers to the team, the project will most likely fail. Organizational decisions also specify the composition and leader of a team and designate authority and responsibility. If the organizational make-up of the team is not effective, a leader needs to change it.

Informational decisions involve the flow of communications and designate who routinely communicates with whom. We expect routine communication between teams and subordinate teams, but if it is not occurring, then the organization's informational design is flawed or not being used. If your plan is desynchronized and failing, it is often because of inadequate communications. Information flow increases situational awareness. Situational awareness is an understanding of the environment and the ability to predict likely outcomes. If situational awareness is low, the informational process may be at fault. To improve the communications flow in your organization, first understand which team members or subordinate leaders routinely communicate information to whom, and at what frequency. If the leaders are sending information to the wrong person, then the process is inefficient or useless. If the frequency of communications is not correct, the right information will not arrive in time. Knowing who communicates with whom, and at what frequency communications occur, is something every leader should investigate, understand and influence. If the informational set-up of the team is not effective, a leader must change it.

> ### Decision Categories
>
> Organizational—Who works for whom?
> Informational—Who talks to whom?
> Operational—Which course of action to execute?

Operational decisions are the ones that most leaders understand as there is an obvious cause and effect when good or bad decisions are executed. Operational decisions direct the success of every effort. Businesses make hundreds of operational decisions every day. These decisions keep production going, make sales happen, and move projects along to completion, or they do not. Most of these decisions represent tame problems that managers, supervisors and leaders deal with routinely. In almost every operation, however, extraordinary circumstances emerge that evolve as critical or wicked problems. The decision by the CEO of a company to shift direction and start a new project, product, or service could fall into this category. Eisenhower's decision to launch the D-Day invasion is an example of an extraordinary operational decision to solve a wicked problem. Elon Musk's 2013 crisis, where he empowered nearly 500 employees to set aside their normal duties to design and produce Tesla cars, and switched their focus to close existing deals, was an extraordinary operational decision that paid off. If leaders consistently make unsuccessful operational decisions, they should be re-trained or replaced.

Organizational and informational decisions made prior to the start of a project or plan can have a significant influence on the outcome of operational decisions. Leaders who understand that all operational decisions are made in context with organizational and informational structures have a deeper sense of situation awareness. If your team's organizational and informational decisions are faulty, even the best operational decision may not save the day. Effective leaders learn to align their team's operational, organizational and informational decisions to improve how the team decides, organizes and communicates.

Decision-Making Approaches

The first key decision that skilled leaders make is to select how to decide. This choice is easier if the leader has raised their awareness of decision-making, understands the various approaches, and practices them. There are two primary methods of deciding and the choice depends on the time available and the experience of the leader. These two methods are deliberate (analytical decision-making) and intuitive (recognition primed decision-making).

Deliberate decision-making is an intentional process that fosters effective analysis by enhancing application of professional knowledge, logic and judgment. Any team, organization, or business can adopt this method to improve a plan. As part of the deliberate decision-making process, several options should be developed. These options, often called courses of action (COA), can be quantified for comparison, providing the decision-maker with a numerical method to qualify the ultimate choice. The deliberate process usually involves several experts, staff advisors, or department managers, to gather, analyze and prioritize information; create several COAs to achieve the plan; compare the developed courses of action; and then select the best COA. This approach generally follows these steps: 1) recognize and define the problem; 2) analyze the problem, gather facts and make assumptions necessary to determine the scope of the problem; 3) develop several possible alternative solutions or COAs; 4) analyze each COA; 5) compare each COA; 6) select the best COA; 7) and then implement and verify the solution.

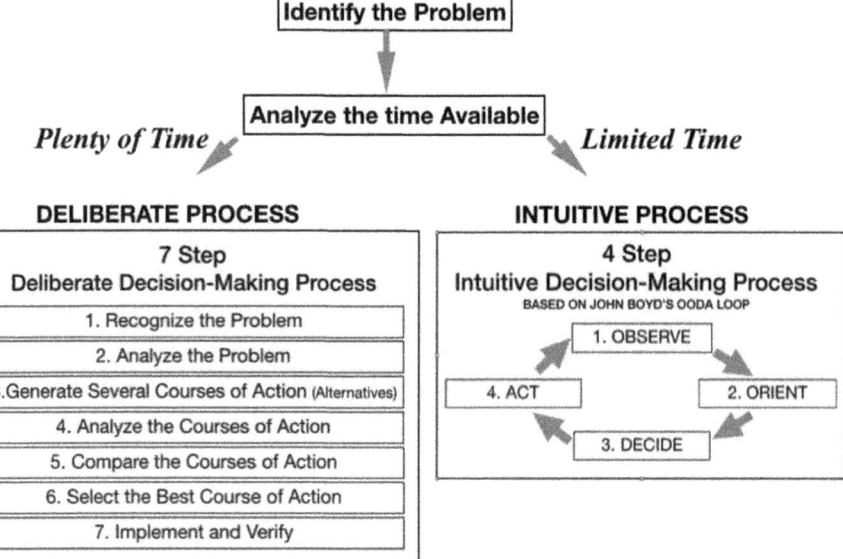

Decision-Making Methods

Deliberate Decision-Making

1. Time is not critical. There is sufficient time to conduct a deliberate analysis and course of action development.
2. The situation is abstract with little pattern recognition.
3. The level of experience of the leader and the team is low.
4. There is a need to justify and "buy into" the decision.
5. The situation requires explicit understanding of the people involved in the planning as the team and leader are new or inexperienced.
6. There is a need to use planning sessions to resolve group conflicts.
7. There is need to find the optimal course of action.

The deliberate method may not be suitable for every decision: it requires ample time and experienced advisors to complete every step. Rushing through the steps without detailed analysis corrupts the value of being deliberate. Time pervades all decision-making. Napoleon Bonaparte said: "I may lose a battle, but I will never lose a minute." Napoleon understood the value of time and he sought to make rapid and decisive decisions. "Too late," is the lament of many indecisive leaders and legions of investors. Often, a complex or uncertain situation causes "analysis paralysis" that results in delayed decisions, or not implementing action until it is too late.

The first step before making any decision, therefore, is to quickly analyze the available time and decide if there is sufficient time for deliberate decision-making. If there is not enough time, or if the advisors developing the plan are inexperienced, the leader should use the intuitive decision-making process. This process is epitomized by the Observe–Orient–Decide–Act sequence, also known as the OODA Loop. United States Air Force Colonel John Boyd developed this cycle to help leaders make decisions in time and under pressure. In Boyd's explanation of the OODA loop, he stated: "…in order to win, we should operate at a faster tempo or rhythm than our adversaries—or, better yet, get inside [the] adversary's observation-orientation-decision-action time cycle or loop. Such activity will make us appear ambiguous (unpredictable) thereby generate confusion and disorder among our adversaries—since our adversaries will be unable to generate mental images or pictures that agree with the menacing as well as faster transient rhythm or patterns they are competing against." Boyd believed that rapid decisions are required when time is short and there is insufficient time for a deliberate process.

In the 2013 *Harvard Business Review* article, "Decision Making, Top Gun Style," authors Mark Bonchek and Chris Fussell outlined how Boyd's OODA applies to business:

> Like fighter pilots, they [business leaders] must acquire data, turn data into insight, and then act on that insight. The difference is that modern leaders must enable entire organizations to have this capacity… In the corporate world, organizations are also beginning to create large-scale OODA loops. Social media monitoring is one of the key technologies for creating OODA loops. During the Super Bowl blackout (on February 4, 2013), Oreo received a lot of attention for its tweet, "You can still dunk in the dark." This didn't happen by accident. Lisa Mann, then VP of Cookies at Oreo-maker Mondelez International (she's since moved up to Senior VP of Global Gum), had set up a "social media command center"—one that would have been very familiar to any special operations team. All of Oreo's agencies and stakeholders were physically and virtually connected. Everyone [was] in place to jump on a real-time marketing opportunity," Mann said. Oreo had designed a system to give it an OODA advantage.

According to Bonchek and Fussell, you beat the competition by observing the situation, orienting leaders on specified goals, deciding swiftly, and then implementing the decision faster than your opponent. You do this by using the OODA loop in situations where time is fleeting. When a firefighter arrives at a fire, and is faced with a life and death decision, there is no time to waste. The firefighter faces a situation where every second counts. A veteran firefighter, using an intuitive OODA loop process, observes the fire, assesses the risks, orients key firefighting assets to fight the blaze, decides how to rescue the tenants, and acts in time to save their lives. The success of rapid decision-making is determined by the firefighter's skill, training and experience. If the firefighter is untrained or inexperienced, a hasty decision puts everyone in peril. Waiting for the house to burn down, without acting, is also catastrophic. Training and experience are required to develop this "sixth sense" to make rapid decisions. Miyamoto Musashi, the samurai discussed in Chapter 3, wrote in *A Book of Five Rings,* "You must train day and night in order to make quick decisions." In unskilled, untrained and inexperienced hands, hasty decisions often fail. With trained and experienced leaders, rapid decision-making is the key to success in dynamic situations. To gain experience, leaders must practice making decisions with limited time and incomplete information.

To those in business today, the future belongs to the fast. Agile leadership is a culture that adapts to deal with change. Our high-tech world, driven by ubiquitous communication and ever-accelerating computing power, requires engaged, interactive and adaptive leadership. LinkedIn is an example of a company that routinely uses an OODA loop style of decision-making to upgrade its product. A team at LinkedIn observes what customers are doing in real-time and follows these trends closely. In one case, the team used the collected data to add an address feature that customers wanted. This generated more users who joined, thereby expanding the LinkedIn customer base. In short, organizations that adopt Boyd's OODA loop decision-making cycle can learn to think and act faster than their competition and seize fleeting opportunities. When you can minimize the time it takes to cycle through the OODA loop, you will observe, orient, decide and act faster than your competition, often making them look as if they are moving in slow motion. This intuitive decision-making process provides a "good enough solution" in time, when there is not enough time for the deliberate decision-making process.

Intuitive Decision-Making

1. Recognize the pattern and apply a counter-pattern.
2. In an unfamiliar situation where there is no distinct pattern, quickly analyze several probable COAs to select a workable COA from experience.
3. Combine scenarios one and two; a novel solution is visualized, chosen and then executed.

An excellent study on the intuitive decision-making process, also known as Recognition Primed Decision-making (RPD), was conducted by author Dr. Gary Klein, titled *Sources of Power, How People Make Decisions*. Klein's approach is like Boyd's as it involved studying people who decided in dynamic situations and under the pressure of limited time. He identified three fundamental decision-making scenarios: 1) Recognized situations are matched with typical actions to facilitate rapid decisions resulting in well-known outcomes; 2) An unfamiliar situation forces the decision maker to analyze probable COAs to select a workable COA from the depth of his or her experience; and 3) Combining scenarios one and two, a novel solution is visualized and chosen. The key to the effectiveness of either the OODA loop or the RPD is the experience of the decision maker. As Klein wrote: "Intuition depends on the use of experience to recognize key patterns that indicate the dynamics of the situation." Experienced decision makers recognize the pattern they are facing and apply a counter-pattern solution. The human brain works by pattern recognition, and each of us uses this ability hundreds of times each day as we decide on a myriad of issues. The more novel and complex the situation, however, the more experience in similar situations comes to play. It is very difficult for inexperienced decision makers, unskilled in the intuitive decision-making process and untrained in their craft, to make effective intuitive decisions in time. This is one reason why the best leaders train, teach and mentor their team members rather than engage in the common practice of just hiring and firing employees. The very best hire for attitude, train for skill, and consistently coach their team members in how to make timely, correct decisions.

Intuitive Decision-making

1. Time is critical. There is limited time available to plan deliberately and there is an urgent need to find a workable course of action as soon as possible.
2. Events are fast-changing, the situation is dynamic, but there are recognizable patterns occurring that a well-trained leader can identify.
3. The level of experience of the leader and team is high, and the leader is trained and confident.
4. The team trusts the leader and they implicitly buy into the decision, understanding that a decision must be made in time or the opportunity is lost.
5. There is little inter-group conflict.
6. There is implicit understanding between the leader and the team.
7. There is an urgent requirement to decide quickly and apply a good enough decision in time to make a difference.

There are no simple recipes for perfect decision-making. The deliberate and intuitive decision-making processes each have advantages if applied to the right situations and disadvantages when used in the wrong circumstances. Time is the central element. The leader's ability to analyze the time available, and choose either an analytical or an intuitive decision-making approach, is often the most important element in decision-making. "Too late" is often the lament of the loser. A famous 18th-century Russian general, Alexander Vasilyevich Suvorov, expressed the notion of the value of time in this way: "Time is the most valuable of all ... Money is dear; human life is still dearer, but time is dearest of all." Or as the great early 20th-century inventor and entrepreneur Thomas Edison said: "Time is really the only capital that any human being has, and the only thing he can't afford to lose." To raise your leadership, improve your awareness of how to analyze the time available to make decisions.

How to Plan

Planning is the skill to project your thoughts forward in time (when), space (where), and purpose (reason) to develop a course of action that will accomplish your goal. Planning involves the ability to visualize a situation, define a desired end state, and lay out effective ways to bring that end state into reality. Planning organizes, positions, and readies you to take advantage of a future situation. Since the future is unknown, all planning is speculative. Good planners reduce risk and uncertainty by calculation and the most up-to-date understanding of the situation. Sun Tzu, the ancient Chinese sage of war, said: "With many calculations one can win; with few one cannot. How much less the chance for victory has one who makes none at all!" This is the essence of planning. In personal decision-making, business or war, your knowledge of yourself and your team, the situation (which includes the competition), and your ability to use the time you have, form the basis for all actions. Once you understand all three elements: 1) yourself and your team; 2) the situation; and 3) the time available, you have the basis to develop an effective plan. Maximize the value of time and you can take advantage of fleeting opportunities. If you are lacking insight in any of these areas, gather as much data in the time available to plug these information gaps. Every effective leader understands that there will never be perfect information, and seldom will there be an abundance of time, especially when faced with critical and wicked problems.

One way to address planning is to clarify what you know. I call this the "Four Knows": know the situation and timing; know the environment; know yourself; and know your competition. Knowing the timing involves understanding when actions must occur. Knowing yourself and the competition is self-explanatory. Knowing the situation is comprehending the topography of the human landscape and the real-world setting. If you do not understand any of these four, your chances for success are nil. If you know only one, your plan has a one in four chance of success. If you know only two, a 50 percent chance. Know three and your chances increase. Knowing all four is the pinnacle of good planning, but with all actions in human relations, business and war, the decisive factor is what you know in each quadrant in time to decide. No quadrant will be known at 100 percent, but the higher the level of comprehension the better. Perfect information, 100 percent clarity in all quadrants, is impossible. Leaders must learn to make decisions with limited information. Understanding the quadrants of the Four Knows raises your leadership awareness and can improve your plans.

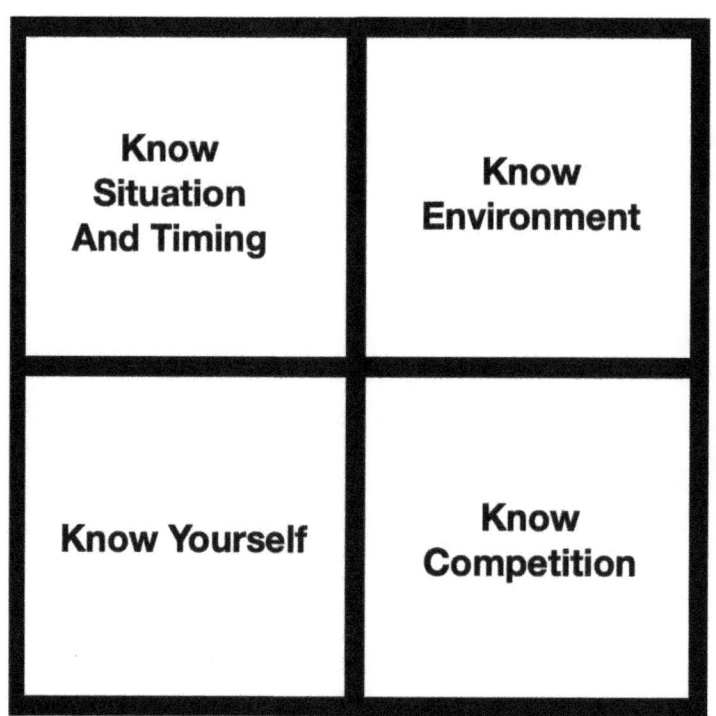

The "Four Knows" of Effective Planning

Planning is vital, and plans provide a point of departure to get the mission accomplished. Much can occur after publishing a plan. Relying only on plans invites failure, or as Eisenhower said: "Plans are nothing. Planning is everything." By this, Eisenhower meant that the team will learn through the planning process and can identify when the plan requires changing, as every plan inevitably does. The leader and team will use the knowledge they learned in developing the plan to adapt the plan to the new circumstances. But what if the situation changes, and the senior leader is not present to make the crucial decision to adjust the plan, and only a subordinate leader is available? Should the subordinate act, or stand by, execute as planned, and watch things fail? Since the plan describes one way to accomplish a mission and represents the best concept to accomplish a task before execution, what do you do during rapidly changing situations when you cannot get a decision from your leader in time?

Planning Format

A Simple Format for any Organization

1. Situation (What we need to know to understand the Mission and achieve the End State).
2. Mission (Who, What and When).
3. Execution and Leader's intent:
   Intent = Purpose, Key Tasks, End State.
   Execution = How we will achieve the End State.
4. Administration and Logistics (Resource Management).
5. Leadership and Control (Where the leader will be at critical points in the plan and what information is critical to inform the leader when changes are required).

An adept leader adjusts the plan to fit the situation and does not try to force the plan to work when the situation has changed and the original plan no longer applies. Making good decisions in rapidly changing circumstances requires adaptive thinking. Adaptive thinking is an agile mindset that requires the mental agility to adjust to changing conditions with appropriate and timely actions. The best plans synchronize actions in time, space, and purpose, but all plans are made before the action starts and often with stale information.

Dynamic situations require fluid thinking. Sticking to a rigid plan that no longer fits the situation is a recipe for failure. When the famous boxing champion Mike Tyson was asked about his plan to win the match against Evander Holyfield, he famously said: "Everyone has a plan until they get punched in the mouth." Tyson knew that plans seldom last past first contact with the competition. As the situation changes, winning leaders adapt and change the plan to fit the circumstances.

In fluid situations, it is difficult for subordinate leaders to react to changes in the plan without general guidance to focus their actions. The means to do this is for the leader to articulate a clear and succinct "leader's intent." Intent describes what constitutes success to empower subordinates to act with disciplined initiative when things don't go according to plan. A crisp intent statement unifies action and produces harmony when there is insufficient time for subordinate leaders to ask for further guidance or instruction. Boyd believed that harmony was the power to perceive or interact with apparently disconnected events or entities in a connected way. Armies, businesses and nations have failed when they force a plan to work in a situation that has changed, and the plan no longer applies. It disrupts harmony. To overcome this, a clearly articulated intent can produce this harmony.

> ### Plans Are Nothing
>
> "Plans are nothing. Planning is everything."
> By this, Eisenhower meant that leaders will learn through planning and when the plan fails, they will use the knowledge they learned in developing the plan to rapidly change and adapt the plan to the new circumstances.

Developing an intent for every mission is a powerful leadership tool. Intent explains the purpose behind what must be done and develops a framework to accomplish the mission in all cases, no matter how the situation changes. A clearly articulated statement of intent expresses the purpose behind a plan so that others can act toward that goal without the need for constant communication. If the leader has trained subordinate leaders and developed a culture where they then execute disciplined action on their own, guided by the leader's intent, the team's decision-making cycle (their OODA loop) will speed up. For example, a soccer team that waits for their coach to direct their every move during the conduct of a game, will inevitably lose. The experienced soccer team learns the coach's intent through constant drill, practices, and an understanding of the coach's strategy. When you dramatically expand the parameters of competition, the rules of the game, into the environment of business and war, the need to issue a clear intent and train a culture of leadership is even more pronounced.

Most plans detail how to accomplish the mission. The intent explains the reason why. If the situation changes and everyone on the team understands the "intent," then the leader, subordinate leaders, and team members can react with coherence to secure the goal in a different way. The mission is still achieved, only the "how" changes. Time is a factor in all forms of human endeavor. We never have enough time. Winning time in war is winning battles. The same is true for business. In business, winning time is winning business. Coming out with a new product or a killer app before the competition is often the difference between success and failure in the marketplace. If you beat your competition to the battlefield, or the marketplace, you generate options that can act in your favor. The faster a leader can make a good decision, the better for all. Issuing a clear intent to subordinate leaders and team members improves your decision-making and is a unifying concept to shape the direction of effort, harmonizing the required team actions. Since decision-making enables effective leadership, improving your ability to decide raises your leadership. Skill in issuing intent is something every leader can practice and learn.

Leader's Intent/Commander's Intent

Purpose: A clear explanation of the purpose of the action, project or mission.
Key Tasks: List the vital tasks that must be accomplished to achieve the purpose.
End State/Win State: A clear visualization of the final outcome and what success looks like.

In the United States Army, we train leaders to operate in uncertain circumstances by understanding the Commander's Intent. A simple definition of intent, applied to the military and business world is: "The Commander's Intent clearly articulates the Purpose, Key Tasks and End State (Win State) of the operation or project. Commander's Intent is a nested concept based on the higher organization's intent and seeks to fulfill the purpose of that higher intent." The concept is to educate, and subsequently empower, lower-level initiative through an understanding of the higher-level intent. Every moment that you are ahead of your competition during the decision-making cycle provides you a distinct advantage. Leader's Intent, developed through consistent practice, will create a higher trust among all levels of the organization to form a culture of initiative and disciplined freedom of action. Whether we call this Leader's Intent, or Commander's Intent, leaders who master this ability add a powerful tool to their leadership toolbox.

Plans are merely a basis for changes. This is true for every endeavor. As Eisenhower's decision on when to launch D-Day illustrates, no plan survives contact with reality. When things do not go according to plan, leaders must quickly recognize that the plan is failing and act decisively. Leaders who understand and issue clear intent empower subordinate leaders and team members to act according to changing circumstances and make decisions when seeking additional guidance is impracticable or impossible. The alternative is to do nothing and watch the effort collapse.

Armies, businesses, and nations have been ruined when a leader tries to force a plan to work in a situation that has changed, and the plan no longer applies. Extraordinary business leaders understand the value of Commander's Intent as much as those in the military. In "Manage Uncertainty with Commander's Intent," a 2010 article in the *Harvard Business Review* by author Chad Storlie: "The role of Commander's Intent is to empower subordinates and guide their initiative and improvisation as they adapt the plan to the changed battlefield environment." The basic framework for this intent is to understand the Task, Purpose, and End State (or Win State) of the leader or organization above you. Articulating intent is a powerful leadership skill. Team members that understand and receive clear intent can exercise disciplined initiative.

Deciding is the essence of leadership. Leaders able to plan and decide are invaluable. Extraordinary leaders think and decide faster than their opponents. Through study and practice, you can master this and become skilled at decision-making. On the eve of D-Day, General Eisenhower's leadership was decisive. In a similar fashion, Elon Musk, who operates five or more companies at a time, knows how to learn from mistakes and decide in time. If he fails to decide in time, his companies will falter. To raise your ability to plan, improve your awareness of planning methods and Leader's Intent. To improve your decision-making, practice making decisions under pressure. Create scenarios and involve your team in developing solutions. When you get good at this, put a time limit on coming to a decision and writing out a plan. Time spent in training your team to make plans and decisions can raise individual and team leadership levels.

Where Leaders Should Be to Make Good Decisions

Once you issue a plan, and every team member is off executing their assigned responsibilities, what do you do next? You monitor and facilitate the plan. Can you make timely decisions without leaving your office? As you have learned by now, leadership is a dynamic process. If you intend to influence the action, then you must be at the right place at the correct time to make accurate and timely course corrections. Where is the right place when extraordinary operational decisions must be made? The answer to this important question is simple and routinely misunderstood.

First, make sure you are involved in the planning process and involve the people who will execute the plan. If you do not participate, and have someone else draft the plan, you will miss an important opportunity to learn about your people, the situation and the competition. When you are involved in the planning, you can articulate a clear intent and be with the planners to inspire the team. Furthermore, if the people who are going to execute the plan help make the plan, they will have "skin in the game" and will support accordingly.

Once the plan is completed and issued the real work begins. A plan is merely an idea. Leaders have to turn these ideas into actions. Plans often fail for lack of disciplined execution. Leaders can observe and influence actions better if they are located at the critical points in time and space where events happen. Even the best laid plans can be sent awry by circumstances. The more complex the environment, and the more proficient the competition, the higher probability that the plan will unravel. Every leader must understand and expect this. The precept, "plans are merely a basis for changes," expresses the idea that plans are best used to provide a general direction, but not the exact path, or schedule, to success. You must adapt, improvise and overcome when things do not go according to the plan.

To bring maximum authority and responsibility to decide complex problems, the leader must be present at the right place and time. With practice, a leader can learn how to identify the foremost decision points of any project, determine the times of greatest risk, and know in advance where to place himself or herself for optimal control. First, study the plan thoroughly, and pose "what if" questions to yourself. Identify where, when, and under what conditions may the plan bend, crack, or fail. These critical times and places become your decision points. If you can recognize the most likely decision points in your planning process, then you can estimate the best time and place to be to influence the unfolding action. Know your plan, discern your decision points, and you will be at the right place to act in time.

Nearly All Plans Change

If plans always went as written, if every project timeline unfolded according to the preconceived schedule, there would be no need for leaders to make any decisions after launching a plan.

Asking "what if" questions at critical points in any planning process is the fundamental precept of "Red Teaming." Red Teaming, as discussed in Chapter 4, is a planning tool where you, or a designated individual or team, plays the role of the competition and acts in an adversarial fashion by highlighting the most likely counteractions, weaknesses and obstacles. Red Teaming can strengthen both the planning effort and the final plan. Historian and strategist Liddell Hart said: "A plan, like a tree, must have branches—if it is to bear fruit. A plan with a single aim is apt to prove a barren pole." If decision points are discovered by Red Teaming the plan, branch plans can be developed in advance and are ready for execution when the opportunity arises, enabling your team to quickly adapt to new and surprising situations. Red Teaming can be of tremendous value in developing flexible decision-making. This may sound like a sixth sense, but it is merely focused thinking about the most likely and most dangerous possibilities. Using the insights gained through aggressive Red Teaming, you can develop into a leader who is at the decision point, at the correct time, and renders the proper decision that leads to success.

Raising your decision-making awareness raises your ability to lead. Confidence in deciding in time comes with practice. Character, competence and commitment remain central to effective decision-making. If any of these areas are anemic, your ability to decide will suffer. You must believe in what you are doing, focus on a solution, use your creative talents to adapt as the circumstance requires, and then never give up. As American author and poet Walter D. Wintle famously said:

If you think you are beaten, you are

If you think you dare not, you don't,

If you like to win, but you think you can't

It is almost certain you won't.

If you think you'll lose, you're lost

For out of the world we find,

Success begins with a fellow's will

It's all in the state of mind.

Leaders show the team the path to success. They do this by planning and making correct, timely, decisions. Deciding is not easy, but it is much harder if you lack a mental framework to visualize how to decide; how to plan; and how to communicate your intent to those you lead. We expect our leaders to communicate effectively. Planning and deciding in the proper time accelerates, synchronizes and harmonizes the team's ability to accomplish any task. As Shakespeare said in his play *Henry V*: "All things are ready, if our minds be so." With practiced decision-making, thoughtful planning, understanding problem sets (tame, critical and wicked), using Leader's Intent, and knowing how to be at the decisive point at the right time, you can be a leader who empowers your team and the pathfinder who shows them the way.

Chapter Summary

1. Decision-making is the key to effective leadership. If a leader is exceptional at motivating, organizing and inspiring people, but cannot make decisions, people will find another leader.

2. Optimism and pessimism are infectious. Leaders must guard against being too optimistic or too pessimistic. These emotions spread more rapidly from the higher echelons of leadership downward than in any other direction.

3. There are three problem sets that all decision makers should understand: Tame, Critical and Wicked. Knowing which problem set you are addressing improves your chances of success.

4. There are three broad categories that impact every decision: organizational, informational, and operational. These decisions frame the success or failure of all organizations.

5. There are two primary methods of making decisions: deliberate (analytical decision-making) and intuitive (recognition primed decision-making). The choice of which to use depends on the time available, the experience of the leader and the organizational level of the decision.

6. Planning is the skill to project your thoughts forward in time, space and purpose to develop a course of action (COA) that will accomplish your goal. Planning involves the ability to visualize a situation, define a desired end state, and lay out effective ways to bring that end state into reality.

7. Plans seldom work perfectly, and unforeseen circumstances arise to jeopardize the best of plans. When a leader can issue a clear intent, comprising the purpose, key tasks, and end state, he or she can empower subordinate leaders to act decisively, in rapid time, and even without additional instructions, to achieve the desired outcome

NOTES

CHAPTER 7

Rally Points for Challenging Times

Rally Points Help You Mark the Path of Your Leadership Journey

The newly formed American Republic was about to be stillborn. The ideals expressed in the Declaration of Independence were nearly thrown away in the closing days of the American Revolution. After the humiliating defeat of the British Army at Yorktown, Virginia, the British admitted the inevitability of American independence and began to remove their forces from the United States. By March 1783, the fighting was over and negotiations for a final settlement were in process with the British Parliament and King George. Washington bivouacked his army at Newburgh, New York, and prepared to renew military operations if the negotiations failed. At Newburgh, the Army had little to do but wait for the final signing of a peace treaty. During this time, Washington's soldiers grumbled about long-promised wages that remained unpaid. The soldiers who had fought for eight long years received little or no pay from Congress. Frustrated with a Congress the soldiers viewed as uncaring and unengaged, their anger grew. Congress, however, had almost no money to pay anyone. In 1783, Congress was operating under the "Articles of Confederation and Perpetual Union," started in 1776, but not formally ratified by all 13 states until 1781. The Articles of Confederation bound the states in a loose union but gave little power to the Congress. It also specifically denied Congress the right to levy taxes from the states. In fact, Congress was at the mercy of the states for all revenue, and the states were unwilling to pay. With nearly no money, Congress could not pay the Army, let alone the pensions they had promised to the soldiers who fought the war.

Because of this injustice, a group of American officers, with the support of General Horatio Gates, a senior general who desired to replace Washington as commander, petitioned for the pay that Congress had pledged. Gates seized the passion of the moment and sent the petition without informing

Washington. Congress denied the petition. Washington learned of the petition from Congress, after the fact.

General Washington sympathized with his officers and men over Congress' unfulfilled promises. He respected their sacrifice, but he maintained a steady resolve to obey the orders of the civilian government. He had argued vigorously on his soldiers' behalf, over the intervening eight years of conflict, for Congress to keep its commitments to the men. Washington loved his soldiers, knew firsthand how courageously they had fought against terrible odds and understood that his men felt betrayed. He did not underestimate the passion of his officers and soldiers concerning Congress' unfulfilled promises. Several officers openly talked about their right to force Congress to pay past wages and of "the injuries the troops have received" from the lack of Congressional support. One officer, Lewis Nicola, even hinted that America would be better off if the Army declared Washington as king. Washington learned of this and replied in writing to Nicola's proposal: "No incident in the course of the war in me triggers painful feelings as your message, that such ideas are circulating in the army, as you expressed it."

It would have been easy for Washington to agree with his soldiers, denounce Congress for their failures, promise to march on the capital in Philadelphia, and demand what was due his men at the point of a bayonet. Many a general in history had done just this and then declared themselves dictator or king. Possibly a Caesar or a Napoleon would have led a revolt against Congress, but not Washington. He was made of finer stuff. Washington was a leader who believed in liberty and held true to his principles.

Passions flared and the crisis in civil–military control came to a head when a group of officers led by Major John Armstrong published anonymous letters, now called the "Newburgh Addresses," demanding a meeting to discuss the payment issue and possibly the replacement of Washington with Gates. The letters urged the use of whatever means necessary to secure the Army's just recompenses. They declared that, if they were not paid as the Congress had promised, the Army would refuse to fight to protect Congress if the British attacked. The Newburgh Address declared that the Army would not disband until Congress met its promises. In the extreme case, these letters supported bypassing Congress and establishing a military dictatorship.

The officers organizing the effort articulated in the Newburgh Addresses called for an open meeting on March 12, 1783. As soon as Washington learned of this meeting, he cancelled it. Undeterred, the conspirators scheduled another meeting. On March 15, the unauthorized meeting formed in the "New Building," a wooden hall in the Newburgh Camp. General Gates presided over the opening of the meeting, and nearly all the Army's officers were present. Washington was not invited. The organizers of the meeting felt that Washington would not act against Congress on their behalf. The Army was in open mutiny and acting without the consent of their commanding general.

The meeting had just begun, when to everyone's surprise, Washington entered the room and asked to address the assembly of officers. Washington's demeanor showed that he understood the challenge against his authority. Gates quietly relinquished the floor. Washington stood in front of his officers. He paused, gazed upon them, and saw the frustration and anger on their faces. He took out a sheet of paper with prepared comments that he had written in his own hand and addressed his men. He spoke about their duty as soldiers and reminded them how long and hard they had fought for their cause. He spoke for about three minutes; everyone in the room remained silent. Despite his great communication skills, his words did not move them. They listened respectfully but remained unconvinced.

Washington stopped speaking and the room went silent. He placed his prepared comments on a table. After a moment, he reached into his pocket and pulled out another letter, written by Congress to explain their financial problems and expressing their efforts to support the Army. Handwritten in small script, the words were hard for Washington to read. In the dim light inside the New Building, Washington fumbled in his breast pocket for a set of reading glasses. His men had seen their tireless, gallant general lead them in dozens of battles and always brave the enemy's fire. Washington had unfailingly been at the front of the fight, and on several occasions, had bullets riddle his coat, but he always emerged from the thick of battle uninjured. He had led the Army and stayed with his men during eight long years of war, never leaving their side. He served for no pay and expected Congress only to reimburse him for reasonable expenses. Washington's character was above reproach, and he was the hero of every soldier in the Army.

Washington's officers had never witnessed Washington with reading glasses before. As Washington moved to put on his glasses, he announced: "Gentlemen, you will permit me to put on my spectacles, for I have not only grown gray but almost blind in the service of my country."

Washington was so respected and loved by his officers and his men, it was inconceivable that he should first admonish them and now allow them to see him reduced to wearing glasses. This simple act was the defining moment. The personal strength and esteem of one man, George Washington, saved the Republic. Instantly, the officers gathered in the New Building remembered how much they, and Washington, had sacrificed for the "Glorious Cause of

Liberty" and the independence of the United States. The conspiracy collapsed.

Tears flowed in the eyes of many of his officers. Washington's inspiration had turned their hearts and restored republican values. Every man there realized the personal sacrifices that General Washington had made, and continued to make, for freedom. Washington's sterling character, and his reading glasses, saved the Republic.

The officers voted overwhelmingly to reject the Newburgh Addresses and wholeheartedly followed Washington's wishes to obey the Congress. From this point on, the Army would work on their grievances with Congress and not against the government. A precedent, uncommon in human history, was set. There would be no *coup d'etat* by the Army. In America, the bayonet would not rule; liberty would survive, and a leader of exemplary character, extraordinary competence and unfailing commitment had changed the course of history.

The story of Washington at Newburgh is one that many exceptional leaders understand and can relate to. Leadership is difficult. If leadership were easy, everyone would be a leader. Taking on the mantle of leadership requires that you help others by leading them on the path to achieve the team's goals and missions. Leaders often need rally points along the way to keep them on course. A rally point is a guidepost that helps the leader to reassemble and reorganize if the leader or the team becomes lost or dispersed. Leaders must know which rally point to move to at each phase of the mission should they lose their way. It is easy for leaders to lose their way without discernible rally points.

Leadership Rally Point

A leadership rally point focuses the leader's principles, character, competencies and commitment to achieve a purpose. These rally points are guiding principles that define your leadership. They act as signposts along your leadership journey to help you stay on the path of becoming a better leader.

A leadership rally point focuses the leader's principles, character, competencies and commitment to achieve a purpose. These rally points are guiding principles that define your leadership. They act as signposts along your leadership journey to help you stay on the path of becoming a better leader. What are your rally points?

As with Washington at Newburgh, leaders make the difference between honor or shame, success or failure, and victory or defeat. The best leaders can produce a synergy that transforms teams to be more than the sum of their parts. Without synergy, selfish leaders can destroy teamwork and drive organizations to fail. Leading a team through hardships and disappointment can test your resilience and commitment. Leadership is often demanding, but the challenge offers great rewards. Overcoming setbacks to build and guide a winning team can be an electrifying experience that can inspire others to do much more than they ever thought possible. Winning leaders can improve the well-being of their teammates and increase productivity. In the case of George Washington, it demonstrates they can build a legacy that lasts through the ages.

Leadership Awareness

Raise your leadership awareness through study and seeking opportunities to gain leadership experience. Ultimately, understanding leadership is fundamentally a journey about understanding one's self.

Leadership is a behavioral skill. Raise your leadership awareness through study and seek opportunities to gain leadership experience. Fundamentally, leadership is a journey of self-awareness and service to others. Self-awareness is essential. Service to others, rather than self, improves self-esteem and confidence. There is no greater reward than to unlock your ability to influence, motivate, inspire, and lead people to succeed. In today's competitive, ever-changing and fast-paced world of business, the companies and teams that survive and prosper over the long term are those which are led by people with character, competence and commitment who invest in and develop their people. If people are your team's greatest asset, this approach is logical and smart. Hire and fire organizations seldom grow teams that become more than the sum of their individual members. There may be superstars on the team, but the team is working without synergy and not operating like a "super team" since the focus is short-term, and people consistently move in and out of jobs. Successful organizations strive to attract, grow and nurture leaders who can develop "super teams" for the long run that excel and win.

As I write this final chapter, our planet is experiencing the horrible COVID-19 pandemic, a catastrophe that many see as out of place in our modern world. Many people question how this can happen with all the medical advances humans have made over the centuries. Plagues seem anachronistic in our modern society, but the genuine answer is that our world is still a very dangerous place and "Black Swan" events, like the COVID-19 virus, can still rock the foundations of civilization. This virus has killed hundreds of thousands, infected millions more, and changed the lives of everyone. During this time, fear is common as the knowledge to make informed decisions is scarce. Many people around the world feel isolated as they are social distancing or living in quarantine. People are looking for answers. Stunned by COVID-19, people are looking for leaders to guide them through these unprecedented and stressful times.

Fear is the worst virus. Leadership is the cure. Be a leader. Leaders can generate the action, faith, hope and courage to conquer fear. In times of crisis and challenge, leadership is the vital ingredient. The crucible that the insidious, invisible COVID-19 enemy presents is testing the mettle of leaders and people around the globe. It demands leadership at every level, from families, communities, cities and nations. The leaders caught in the maelstrom of this crucible will have to earn the trust of those who follow them. They will have to be selfless in their efforts to save lives, maintain economies and shorten the duration of infection. The very best leaders across the globe must cooperate and act with foresight to counter this "wicked" problem. Short-term fixes often cascade into bigger problems. Foresight is the ability to fix problems in the short term while developing more permanent solutions for the long run. Leaders with foresight are in great demand, particularly in times like these.

> ### Fear is the Worst Virus
>
> Fear is the worst virus. Leadership is the cure. Be a leader. Leaders can generate the faith, hope and courage to conquer fear.

During an even more trying time for the United States, Abraham Lincoln faced a very wicked problem. The American Civil War was the most destructive and bloodiest war the United States ever endured. In the end, approximately 655,000 soldiers died from both sides, and untold civilians were killed in the fighting, with a total figure of over a million casualties (dead, wounded and missing). This number is greater than the entire sum of all the wars America has ever fought, including World War I and World War II. In the last months of the Civil War, there was little doubt that the Confederacy was doomed to lose. Many leaders in the Union Government in Washington pressed President Lincoln to crush the South, hang their leaders, and enact a terrible and swift revenge. Lincoln, however, was a statesman, not a politician. Like Washington, Lincoln was endowed with tremendous foresight. He saw the United States as one nation, not just North and South. In his second inaugural address, delivered on March 4, 1865, Lincoln sought to set the tone for the peace to come and to reintegrate the Southern states into the Union:

> With malice toward none, with charity for all, with firmness in the right as God gives us to see the right, let us strive on to finish the work we are in, to bind up the Nation's wounds, to care for him who shall have borne the battle and for his widow and his orphan, to do all which may achieve and cherish a just and lasting peace among ourselves and with all nations.

In this address, and by his actions, Lincoln demonstrated his genius for foresight, looking beyond the current problem to solve the greater challenge in the future, to "bind up the Nation's wounds" and make the United States whole again. In word and in deed, Lincoln was an exemplary leader who knew how to address a "wicked" problem.

Foresight

Foresight is the ability to fix problems in the short term while developing more permanent solutions for the long run.

The COVID-19 virus is a prime example of a wicked problem. There is no easy solution, and any answers to the challenges posed by this emergency will only be solved by using all three types of problem-set approaches. Some things, like washing your hands thoroughly and social distancing, are solved through a "tame" or procedural method. Other issues that are time-sensitive and difficult, like moving healthcare providers and supplies to infected areas, represent a "crisis" problem-set and will be solved by a leader executing command. The overall defeat of the virus, however, is truly a wicked problem set and will require "unity of effort" from leaders across the globe. These leaders will have to impel others, over whom they have no authority or responsibility, to work together to achieve a common goal of defeating the virus. To accomplish this, they will need foresight; the talent of solving problems in the short term and for the long run. During their journey to solve this wicked problem, these leaders, our pathfinders, will need rally points to keep them on the path to success.

As defined earlier, a leadership rally point is a mental trigger to focus the leader's principles, character, competencies and commitment toward a purpose. These rally points contain guiding ideas that define your leadership. They act as signposts along your leadership journey to help you keep on the path of being a better leader. What are your rally points? How are you raising your leadership level every day? The following seven rally points provide you with additional tools that can assist you in raising your leadership awareness and sharpen your leadership ability.

1. Rise. You will rise to the level of your leadership. Leaders are made by learning and experience. Learning how to lead is a journey. You can influence your journey by aggressively seeking knowledge and experience. Volunteer and choose to lead whenever you can to gain experience. Read to lead to gain awareness. Embrace a thirst for knowledge with focus and passion. Reading will help you gain knowledge. Write to sharpen your thoughts. Reflect on your actions at the end of each day. Leadership wisdom is the combination of knowledge and experience. With only knowledge you may be wise, but potentially not very useful. Become a pathfinder, not just a path-follower. Leaders blaze trails for others. Leaders know that there is no single formula for success. Leaders that can create a synergy that is more powerful than the sum of the individual parts are leaders that will always be in demand. Leadership is an art. Leadership matters and teamwork wins.

> ### Rise
>
> **You will rise to the level of your leadership. Leadership is an art. Leadership matters and teamwork wins.**

2. Courage. Fear is a reaction; courage is a decision. Leaders decide on courage. All of us face fears. Leadership is action under fear; fear of failure, fear of harm, fear of death. Leaders overcome these fears by deciding on courage and boldly facing the problem. Leaders cycle through the fear faster than others, overcome it, choose courage, and act. Mark Twain said that "Courage is resistance to fear, mastery of fear—not absence of fear." Aristotle called courage the first virtue, because it makes all of the other virtues possible. Courage is a fundamental prerequisite for effective leadership. Courage is not necessarily heroism. Courage is acted on every day, in small things and large. Courage is the determination to do what must be done, in spite of the fear and risk it may entail. If you want to overcome your fears, take a tip from American philosopher Ralph Waldo Emerson: "Do the thing you fear, and the death of fear is certain." Fear is a reaction; courage is a decision. Decide on courage.

Courage

Fear is a reaction; courage is a decision. Leaders decide on courage.

3. Character. Character is destiny. Character is a habit, reinforced consistently by small acts that grow into a powerful, personal force of will and example. Character portrays your nature as a leader. Are you trustworthy, selfless and energetic, or are you a liar, greedy and slothful? Character is based on principles and values. Principles are the fundamental truths or propositions that serve as the foundation for your system of beliefs, behaviors, and reasoning. More than values, principles can serve as your compass, designating true north, and guiding you along your leadership journey. "Before we can stand out," author Simon Sinek said, "we must first get clear on what we stand for." Your core values define what you stand for, what you would fight for, and what you would sacrifice everything for. Values help define your individual leadership traits as they express your unique character. When you consistently live by your personal, core values, and when they are congruent with your actions, you move closer to fulfillment. Your personal character is the sum of your principles and values. Developing a sterling character, being known as a person of integrity, is priceless. Integrity, therefore, above all things. Once you lose it, you will never fully recover. Integrity is integral to earning trust. No one knows if they can count on you until they see you act consistently, consecutively and coherently, especially in the face of challenges and stress. Leaders build trust by matching their words with their deeds. Managers do things right. Leaders do things right and also do the right things. Marcus Aurelius said: "If it is not right, do not do it, if it is not true, do not say it." Character is destiny. Develop your character and reap a destiny.

Character

Character is destiny. Character is a habit, reinforced consistently by small acts that grow into a powerful personal force of will and example.

4. Competence. Competence is a decisive rally point on your leadership path. Can you do the work? Are you competent at what you expect others to do?

If you do not know what needs to be accomplished, or if you cannot do the work, why should anyone follow you? If you lack the knowledge required of the task, find someone to teach you. If you don't know how, learn how. Study your craft to learn what you are lacking and understand enough to know the difference. Leaders do not have to be the best at everything—that is impossible—but they must be able to do the work. Most leaders are generalists who can recognize enough to effectively apply the right talents of their team members to accomplish the mission at hand. To be a leader, a pathfinder, you must know the way and show the way. As author Robert Heinlein wrote: "A human being [a leader] should be able to change a diaper, plan an invasion, butcher a hog, conn a ship, design a building, write a sonnet, balance accounts, build a wall, set a bone, comfort the dying, take orders, give orders, cooperate, act alone, solve equations, analyze a new problem, pitch manure, program a computer, cook a tasty meal, fight efficiently, die gallantly. Specialization is for insects." This means that leaders must know enough about their craft, and what it means to be a human being, to relate effectively to their teammates by motivating, inspiring and directing them to success. Improving your competency will also help hone your decision-making skills. If you consistently make bad decisions, your leadership will fail. Competency helps you discern between correct and incorrect choices. It does not matter how new a leader you are, or how accomplished your organization is. A competent leader can be effective with a mediocre team, while an ineffective leader can demoralize the best-trained organization. Effective leaders, therefore, understand the importance of working every day to be competent. They learn, practice and discipline themselves to maximize their time to increase their competence in the skills that count.

Competence

Leaders must know enough about their craft, and what it means to be a human being, to relate effectively to their teammates and know how to motivate, inspire, and direct them to success.

5. Commitment. Commitment overcomes obstacles. Fully commit to your goal and cause. Adapt, improvise and overcome. Attitude is the engine of commitment, and this combination trumps everything. Your heart and brain must be in the game. If your attitude is weak, how can you be strong?

If your attitude is defeatist, how can you win? If you think you are lacking, you are right; you will fail. If you believe you can succeed, you will. George Washington said: "Ninety-nine percent of failures come from people who make excuses." Leaders turn obstacles into opportunities. This is not about simply being optimistic or Pollyannaish. It is about determination and adaptation that, if you are blocked, you do not hesitate to continue to move forward in a new direction. Author Ryan Holiday describes commitment as "learning to be ceaselessly creative and opportunistic." Elon Musk epitomizes this attitude. He challenged the national space agencies with his SpaceX initiative. Despite numerous financial and bureaucratic obstacles, through his sheer determination, he revolutionized America's resurgence as the world's dominant space-faring nation. Elon Musk's determination to never quit is propelling America and humanity to reach for the Moon, Mars and beyond. Learn from these leaders and incorporate their lessons into your own life. Just as others have done in the past, you can imbue those you lead with the determination to succeed. Do not make excuses; find a way or make one. By moving forward, you generate options.

Commitment

Commitment overcomes obstacles. Leaders turn
obstacles into opportunities.
Do not make excuses; commit to succeed.
Find a way or make one. Once you quit, it is over by default.

6. Example. All leadership is by example. The leader is the role model for everyone on the team. Wise leaders strive to make every action a good example for their team members to emulate. They accomplish this though consistent, consecutive and coherent thought and action. Actions, attitude, thoughts and words must be in alignment. It is simply this: say what you mean and do what you say. Words are impactful, thus leaders who communicate the proper words, at the appropriate time, and most importantly, follow up with action, are pathfinders that people will follow despite difficulty, hardship and sacrifice. Do everything you ask of those you lead. The best leaders reflect any accomplishments onto their team; they do not take the credit to try and shine brighter than their teammates; thus, reflect, do not shine. Leadership by example is a fundamental choice with significant ramifications. All leaders build their own leadership framework, one that is either selfless or selfish. Selfish leaders abound. Selfless leaders are rare. Be a selfless leader who serves the team and raises them to succeed.

An example of selflessness is the idea that "leaders eat last." Wise leaders understand this analogy is about putting their teammates ahead of self, showing the importance of each individual member by a simple sacrifice of being last to be served and last to gain the rewards. Such selflessness is always recognized by the team. All leadership is by example. Leaders are judged by how they treat people over whom they have no authority or responsibility for. How you treat people is a window to your soul. If you take responsibility to plan, prepare, and execute so others are inspired to do more than they thought possible, to accomplish things together as a team that they could never achieve separately, then you are leading by example. Leaders set the example by training, coaching and mentoring their teammates to build teamwork and a team identity.

Lead by Example

All leadership is by example. Wise leaders strive to make every action a good example for their team members to emulate. They accomplish this though consistent, consecutive and coherent thought and action.

7. Know yourself and be yourself. Leadership expert Steven Covey expressed it this way: "

> The "Inside–Out" approach to personal and interpersonal effectiveness means to start first with self; even more fundamentally, to start with the most inside part of self—with your paradigms, your character, and your motives… private victories precede public victories, that making and keeping promises to ourselves precedes making and keeping promises to others… it is futile to put personality ahead of character, to try to improve relationships with others before improving ourselves.

Leaders strive to be self-aware. Identify your strengths and weaknesses. Sharpen your strengths and compensate for your weaknesses. To paraphrase President Theodore Roosevelt: "Unless a person is master of their own soul, all other kinds of mastery amount to little." In short, to know yourself, you should know what you stand for, know what you will fight for, and know what you would die for. If you can answer these three questions you will better "know yourself" and can "be yourself" when it matters the most.

Leaders are in great demand and are fundamental to every human endeavor. "We need leaders, and not just political leaders," American historian and Pulitzer Prize-winning author David McCollough said in a *Harvard Business Review* interview in 2008. "We need leaders in every field, in every institution, in all kinds of situations. We need to be educating our young people to be leaders. And unfortunately, that's fallen out of fashion." Later, in 2015, McCollough went on to say: "One of the great lessons of history is that almost nothing of consequence is ever accomplished alone. It's a joint effort. Leadership is about getting people to come together in a joint effort."

Know Yourself

Leaders strive to be self-aware. Know yourself first, then be yourself. Identify your strengths and weaknesses. Sharpen your strengths and compensate for your weaknesses.

You can be a leader, a pathfinder, and make your world better. Leadership is the art of influence. According to General Dwight D. Eisenhower: "The one quality that can be developed by studious reflection and practice is leadership." The leader influences everyone on the team, for better or for worse. A leader with confidence can influence teammates to believe in success. A leader with courage can inspire the same in others. A leader with skill in interpersonal relationships can guide the team to work together and overcome difficulties. Successful leaders demonstrate the character, competence, and commitment to motivate teams to get the job done.

"We are what we repeatedly do," Aristotle wrote. "Excellence, therefore, is not an act but a habit." The best leaders consistently display admirable character, continuously hone their competencies, and constantly reinforce their commitment to the team and the mission. A leader's focus, and selfless dedication to the task at hand, influences others to believe that even the most difficult mission, under severe hardships, can be achieved. Leaders who takes their job seriously, but not themselves, who do not yearn to shine, but strive to reflect, can influence others. A leader who understands that leadership is the art of influence can inspire people to act together as a team to win. Be this kind of leader.

Character, Competence, Commitment

Character, competence, and commitment are needed by anyone who wishes to be a successful leader.

As I mentioned Archilochus earlier in this book, it is worth remembering the quote attributed to him: "We don't rise to the level of our expectations, we fall to the level of our training." Leadership excellence requires constant improvement. Train yourself. Take responsibility for your own leadership growth. The leadership lessons in this book are time-tested, universal and are yours to use. My advice to you is to get into the game. Do not give up and voluntarily take yourself off the field out of fear. Be an independent thinker and reinforce your awareness of leadership by reading every chance you have. Read to lead. Learn from the great thinkers and leaders of the past. When you have the opportunity to lead, step up and take hold of the mantle of leadership. The exceptional leader's journey is one of self-awareness, continual learning and fostering a selfless attitude. Become what you want your team members to be.

If you raise your awareness of leadership, you can raise your leadership, and you can raise your life. Ultimately, the choice is yours: shall you be a pathfinder or a path-follower? You can wait for someone else to take control of your destiny, or you can take charge and chart your own course, for yourself and your team. Leaders change the potential energy of a group into the kinetic energy of a team. You can opt to play it safe and follow the group, or take a risk, summon up the courage, and lead your team to explore new frontiers. Exceptional leaders are pathfinders. Pathfinders learn the path, walk the path, and guide others to the destination. If you take this awareness to heart, your leadership is rising. Good luck on your leadership journey!

Leadership Rising

Raise Your Awareness.
Raise Your Leadership.
Raise Your life.

NOTES

Bibliography

Sources I studied to inspire me to write Leadership Rising *and that I highly recommend you read.*

Books

Ashton, Brodi. *Everneath*. Balzer and Bray, 2012.

Aurelius, Marcus. *The Meditations*. Random House, 2002.

Blanchard, Ken. *One Minute Manager*. Harper Collins, 1981.

Brady, Chris and Orrin Woodward. *Launching a Leadership Revolution, Mastering the Five Levels of Influence*. Business Plus, 2007.

Buzan, Tony. *Mind Map Mastery: The Complete Guide to Learning and Using the Most Powerful Thinking Tool in the Universe*. Watkins Publisher, 2018.

Buzan, Tony and Barry Buzan. *The Mind Map Book*. Plume, Penguin Books, 1993.

Cimino, Al. *Apollo, The Mission to Land a Man on the Moon*. Chartwell Books, 2019.

Clear, James. *Atomic Habits: An Easy & Proven Way to Build Good Habits & Break Bad Ones*. Avery, 2018.

Coram, Robert, *Boyd, The Fighter Pilot Who Changed the Art of War*. Little, Brown and Company, 2002.

Covey, Stephen. *The 7 Habits of Highly Effective People*. Free Press, 1989.

Covey, Stephen M. R, with Rebecca R. Merrill. *The Speed of Trust: The One Thing That Changes Everything*. Simon and Schuster, 2006.

Dalio, Ray. *Principles*. Simon & Schuster, 2017.

Drucker, Peter F., *The Peter F. Drucker Reader: Selected Articles from the Father of Modern Management Thinking*. Harvard Business Review Press, 2016.

Emmons, Robert A. *Thanks! How the New Science of Gratitude Can Make You Happier*. Mariner Books, 2008.

Fitton, Robert A. *Leadership; Quotations form the Military Tradition*. Westview Press, 1994.

Franklin, Benjamin. *The Autobiography of Benjamin Franklin*. Edited by Philip Smith. Dover, Publications, 1996 (Originally published 1791).

Gelb, Michael, J. *How to Think Like Leonardo da Vinci*. HarperCollins Publishers, 2013.

Goleman, Daniel. *Emotional Intelligence: Why It Can Matter More Than IQ*. Bantam, 2005.

Grint, Keith. *Leadership, Management and Command, Rethinking D-Day*. Palgrave Macmillan, 2007.

Gross, Ronald. *Socrates' Way: Seven Keys to Using Your Mind to the Utmost*. Penguin, 2002.

Knowles, Elizabeth, ed. *Oxford Dictionary of Quotations, Third Edition*. Oxford University Press, 1980.

Lewis, C. S. *The Chronicles of Narnia*. Harper Collins, 2001.

Maxwell, John. *The 21 Irrefutable Laws of Leadership: Follow Them and People Will Follow You.* Harper Collins Leadership (10th Anniversary Edition), 2007.

Mondschein, Ken Ph.D. *Ancient Greek Philosophers.* Canterbury Classics, 2018.

Morrison, Grant and artist Frank Quitely. *All-Star Superman.* DC Comics, 2005.

Musashi, Miyamoto. *A Book of Five Rings: The Classic Guide to Strategy.* Translated by Victor Harris. Overlook Press, 1974 (first published 1645 五輪書 [Go rin no sho]).

Musashi, Miyamoto. *The Book of Five Rings, The Classic Text of Samurai Sword Strategy.* Translated by Akikga Yoshiharu and edited by Rosemary Brant. Barnes and Noble, 2003.

Peck, Scott M. *The Road Less Traveled, A New Psychology of Love, Traditional Values, and Spirit.* Touchstone, 1980.

Phillips, Donald T. *The Founding Fathers on Leadership.* Warner Books, 1997.

Rost, Joseph C. *Leadership for the 21st Century.* Praeger, 1993.

Sinek, Simon, *Start With Why, How Great Leaders Inspire Everyone to Take Action.* Portfolio, 2009.

Theodore Roosevelt. *Theodore Roosevelt, His Essential Wisdom.* Edited by Carol Kelly Gangi. Fall River Press, 2013.

Tsouras, Peter G. *Warriors' Words. A Quotation Book, From Sesostris II to Schwarzkopf, 1971 BC to AD 1991.* Cassell Arms and Armor, 1992.

Tzu, Lao. *Tao Te Ching (The Way).* Translated by Stephen Mitchell. Harper Collins, 2009.

Tzu, Lao. *Tao Te Ching, A Book About the Way and the Power of the Way.* Edited and translated by Ursula K. Le Guin. Shambhala, 2011.

Tzu, Sun, *The Art of War.* Translated by Lionel Giles. Dover Publications, 2002.

Tzu, Sun, *The Art of War.* Translated by Samuel Griffith. Oxford University Press, 1971.

Tzu, Sun, and Jessica Hagy. *Art of War Visualized, The Sun Tzu Classic in Charts and Graphs.* Workman Publishing Company, 2015.

US Army, *ADP 6–22 Army Leadership and the Profession.* Headquarters, Department of the Army, 2019.

Vance, Ashlee. *Elon Musk: Tesla, SpaceX, and the Quest for a Fantastic Future.* HarperCollins, 2015.

Warren, Rick. *The Purpose Driven Life, What on Earth Am I Here For?* Zondervan, 2013.

White, Stewart Edward. *Daniel Boone Wilderness Scout.* Garden City Publishing, 1922.

Articles and Online Sources

Cawthon David L. "Aristotle on Leadership— Free from the Tyranny of Passion," *St. Croix Review.* 2001.

Daskal, Lolly. "The 100 Best Leadership Quotes of All Time," *Inc. Magazine.* New York. https://www.lollydaskal.com/leadership/the-100-best-leadership-quotes-of-all-time/ 2021.

Fordham University, "About Donald McGannon," https://www.fordham.edu/info/29822/about_the_mcgannon_center/11739/about_donald_mcgannon 2021.

Mentorphile. "Elon Musk's First Principles Thinking," https://mentorphile.com/2019/03/22/elon-musks-first-principles-thinking/ 2019.

Nair, Praseeda. "Greatest inspirational leadership quotes from famous leaders."

Real Business https://realbusiness.co.uk/20-greatest-inspirational-leadership-quotes-from-famous-leaders/ 2020.

Sukhraj, Ramona, "100 leadership quotes to make you a better manager this year." Impact. https://www.impactplus.com/blog/best-leadership-quotes 2020.

Index

action, 32, 60, 68, 87
Adams, John, 81
Adler, Alfred, 108
advertising, 87
Aldrin, Edwin "Buzz", 79–81
Alexander the Great, 70, 86, 88
American Civil War, 158–9
American Revolution, 1–2, 91, 153–6
Angelou, Maya, 105
Apollo 11 mission, 79–81
Archilochus, 78, 166
Aristotle, 8, 33, 70, 165
    Nicomachean Ethics, 85–6
Armstrong, Maj John, 154
Armstrong, Neil, 79–81
Art of War, The (Sun Tzu), 11–12
Ashton, Brodi: *Everneath*, 100
authority, 130–1
Avengers: End Game (film), 109–10

Bennis, Warren, 23, 100
Berra, Yogi, 32–3
Bethel, Sheila Murray: *Making a Difference: 12 Qualities That Make You a Leader*, 116
Bezos, Jeff, 13
Blanchard, Ken: *The One-Minute Manager*, 27
Bonchek, Mark, 136–7
Boone, Daniel, 1–4, 28
bosses, 24, 27–8
Boyd, Col John, 136–7, 144
Bradley, Gen Omar, 123
Brady, Chris: *Launching a Leadership Revolution, Mastering the Five Levels of Influence*, 70
breathing, 109

Buzan, Tony: *Mind Map Mastery: The Complete Guide to Learning and Using the Most Powerful Thinking Tool in the Universe*, 53

Canfield, Jack, 88
Captain America, 109–10
Carlyle, Thomas, 88
Carter, John C., 23
Cawthon, David L.: "Aristotle on Leadership", 86
character, 70–1, 73–4, 161, 166
Clear, James: *Atomic Habits: An Easy & Proven Way to Build Good Habits & Break Bad Ones*, 41, 117
COAs (courses of actions), 133, 138
cognitive empathy, 107–8
Cohen, William: *The Stuff of Heroes: The Eight Universal Laws of Leadership*, 115
Collins, Michael, 79, 81
Commander's Intent, 145–6
commitment, 78–82, 162–3, 166
communication, 75, 92–3, 131; *see also* listening
compass, 61, *62*, 63, 70
compassionate empathy, 107
competencies, 44, 74–9, 161–2, 166
competition, 12, 140–2, 145, 147
conceit, 102
Confucius, 92
Congress, 153–6
country, 65–6
courage, 160–1
Covey, Steven, 60, 66, 111, 164
    The 7 Habits of Highly Effective People, 63–5

The Speed of Trust: The One Thing That Changes Everything, 89
COVID-19 pandemic, 130, 157–9
critical problems, 129, 132, 159
critical thinking, 75
crucibles, 8–11
cummings, e. e., 23

D-Day landings, 121–8, 132, 146
Dalio, Ray: *Principles*, 65–6
Day, Doris, 104
De Gaulle, Gen Charles, 122
decision-making, 12, 27, 80, 116, 121–8
    and approaches, 132–40
    and categories, 131–2
    and competence, 75, 79, 162
    and emotion, 109
    and planning, 140–9
    and principles, 67
    and problem sets, 128–31
definition, *see* leadership definition
delegation, 75
deliberate decision-making, 133–7, 140
Disney, Walt, 31
Drucker, Peter, 87
duty, 65–6

Edison, Thomas, 140
effectiveness, 26
efficiency, 25–6
Einstein, Albert, 91
Eisenhower, Gen Dwight David "Ike", 128, 143, 165
    and D-Day landings, 121–7, 132, 146
Emerson, Ralph Waldo, 34, 67, 160
Emmons, Robert A.: *Thanks! How the New Science of Gratitude Can Make You Happier*, 105
emotional contagion, 109
emotional empathy, 107–8
empathy, 106–10
end-state, 6, 7
environment, 140–2, 147
envy, 102–3
example, 90–2, 163–4

fear, 158, 160
firefighting, 96, 129, 137

first steps, 3–4
focus, 57–8
following, 112–13
foresight, 158–9
"Four Knows", 140–2
Franklin, Benjamin, 12–15, *16*, 17, 21
Fussell, Chris, 136–7

Gates, Bill, 13
Gates, Gen Horatio, 153–5
Gelb, Michael J.: *How to Think Like Leonardo da Vinci*, 35
Gilgamesh, 99
goals, 7, 21–2, 59, 63; *see also* life goals
Godin, Seth, 89
Golden Circle, 5, *6*, 7
Goleman, Daniel: *Emotional Intelligence Why It Can Matter More Than IQ*, 107–8
gratitude, 104–6
Grint, Keith: *Leadership, Management and Command, Rethinking D-Day*, 128–30
Grisham, John, 13
Gross, Ronald: *Socrates' Way: Seven Keys to Using Your Mind*, 8
guidance, 64–5

habits, 41, 44
Hagy, Jessica: *The Art of War Visualized*, 11
happiness, 34, 102–3, 105–6
harmonizing, 130, 144
Hart, Liddell, 148
Harvey, Steve, 4
Heinlein, Robert, 162
Hemingway, Ernest, 110
Heraclitus, 85, 96
Hill, Napoleon, 12, 59
Hitler, Adolf, 126
Holiday, Ryan, 163
Holyfield, Evander, 144
Homer: *Iliad*, 99
honor, 65–6
hope, 90
Hout, Thomas, 23
How, 5, *6*, 7
humility, 101–4

imaging, *see* visualization
influence, 92–3, 95

informational decisions, 131–2
innovation, 3
integrity, 161
intelligence, 106–8
intent, 144–6
intuitive decision-making, 133–4, 138–40
involvement, 81
Iraq, 73

James, William, 107
Japan, 57–9
jealousy, 102–3
Jesus Christ, 92

Karlgaard, Rich, 48
Kent, Germany, 104
key tasks, 6, 7
King, Martin Luther, 70
Klein, Gary: *Sources of Power, How People Make Decisions*, 138
know yourself, *see* self-awareness
knowledge, 113–15, 140–2, 160
Kojiro, 58
Kwik, Jim, 113

Lao Tzu: *Tao Te Ching* (*The Book of the Way and of Virtue*), 4, 12, 14, 17
Law of the Harvest, 63–4
Lawrence, Scott, 130
Leader's Intent, 145–6
leadership definition, 85–96
learning, 113–15, 166
legacy, 46–7
Leigh-Mallory, AC Trafford, 125
Lewis, C. S., 102
life goals, 33, 41–4
Lincoln, Abraham, 70–1, 81, 158–9
LinkedIn, 137
listening, 110–12
logos, 35, *36*, 37
love, 67

MacArthur, Gen Douglas, 65
McCallum, John S., 112
McCloy, John J., 101
McCollough, David, 165
McGannon, Donald, 87

managers, 24–8, 85
Mandela, Nelson, 13
manipulation, 7, 27, 70
Marcus Aurelius, Emperor, 67, 92, 161
    The Meditations, 22–3, 33
mastery, 12
Maxwell, John, 7, 10, 22, 28, 63, 92, 110
Menander, 21
mentors, 76–8
Michelangelo, 113–14
mind map, 51–3
Montgomery, Gen Bernard, 123
Moon landings, 79–81
motivation, 75, 88–9
Musashi, Miyamoto, 66, 76, 82, 86
    A Book of Five Rings, 57–61, 137
Musk, Elon, 2–4, 13, 26, 32
    and decision-making, 132, 146
    and SpaceX, 163
myths, 99–100

Napoleon Bonaparte, 90, 136
National Aeronautics and Space Administration (NASA), 79–81
natural laws, 63–5
neuroplasticity, 21
Newburgh Addresses, 154–6
Nicklaus, Jack, 59
Nicola, Lewis, 154
Nietzsche, Friedrich, 32

OODA (Observe–Orient–Decide–Act) Loop, 136–8
operational decisions, 132
optimism, 124
organizational decisions, 131–2

panic, 109
pathfinders, 1–2, 13–14, 28
patterns, 138
Peck, M. Scott: *The Road Less Traveled, A New Psychology of Love, Traditional Values, and Spirit*, 111
pessimism, 124
Phillips, Pauline Esther "Popo", 70
philosophy, 57–8, 67, 85
Pitino, Rick, 103

planning, 75, 116, 140–9
Plato, 86
Poor Richard's Almanack (Franklin), 13
power, 64–5
principles, 63–9, 161
problem solving, 75
proficiency, *see* competencies
purpose, *6*, 7–8, 31–5, 48–50, 88

rally points, 156–7, 159–66
Ramsay, Adm Bertram, 123, 125
Ramsay, Dave, 13
Ranger School, 9–10
reading, 113–14, 160, 166
Reagan, Ronald, 89
reaping, 63–4, 67
Red Cross, 31
Red Teaming, 95, 148
reputation, 71, 73
resentment, 105–6
responsibility, 130–1
rise, 160
Robbins, Tony, 41
Rommel, Gen Erwin, 123–4
Roosevelt, Theodore, 12, 88, 164
Rost, Joseph C.: *Leadership for the 21st Century*, 92
Rosten, Leo C., 34
RPD (Recognition Primed Decision-making), 138
Ryan, M. J., 28

samurais, 57–9
schedules, *16*
Schwarzkopf, Gen Norman, 73
Schweitzer, Albert, 91
security, 64–5
self-assessment, 17–18, *19*, 20–4
self-awareness, 157, 164–6
self-deception, 12
self-knowledge, 11–15, 17, 20–3
self-mastery, 57–9
selfishness, 115–16, 157, 164
selflessness, 115–16, 164
Seneca, Lucius Annaeus, 41
service, 157
Shakespeare, William, 23
  Henry V, 149

Sharma, Robin, 60
Sinek, Simon, 4–5, *6*, 7, 28, 92
  and humility, 104
  and principles, 161
situational awareness, 131, 140–5
skills, 44, 74–8
Smith, Lt Gen Walter Bedell, 124
Socrates, 8, 85–6, 93, 95
sowing, 63–4, 67
speaking, 116
Stagg, Grp Capt James M., 122–3, 125
Star Trek, 107–8
starting, 3–4
Stipe, Sgt Larry, 76–8
Storlie, Chad, 146
strategy, 57–8
strengths, 20, 44–5
Sun Tzu, 11–12, 140
superheroes, 99–101
Superman, 100–1
superpowers, 100–1, 116–17
  and empathy, 106–10
  and followers, 112–13
  and gratitude, 104–6
  and humility, 101–4
  and learning, 113–15
  and listening, 110–12
  and selflessness, 115–16
Supreme Headquarters Allied Expeditionary Force (SHAEF), 121–7
Suvorov, Alexander Vasilyevich, 140
synergy, 157

tame problems, 128–9, 132, 159
teaching, 74–8, 86, 114–15
teamwork, 115–16
technology, 74–6
Tedder, ACM Arthur, 123, 125
television, 87
telos, 33–4
Tesla Motors, 2–3, 132
thought, 21–3
time, 22, 66–7
  and decision-making, 133–7, 139–40
  and planning, 140–2, 145–7
training, 76–8
trust, 71–3, 89–90
Tukey, John, 60

Twain, Mark, 4, 12, 160
Tyson, Mike, 144

understanding, *see* empathy
United States Army, 9–10, 73–4, 106, 111, 145–6
   3rd Btn, 32nd Armored Rgt, 76–7
United States Military Academy (West Point), 65–6
United States Navy, 31
unity of effort, 130–1, 159
Urban, Tim, 26

values, 37–40, 161; *see also* principles
Vikings, 99
Virgil: *Aeneid*, 99
virtue, 67
visualization, 57–61, *62*

war, 11–12, 31, 73, 158–9; *see also* American Revolution; World War II
Warren, Rick, 93

The Purpose-Driven Life, 102
Washington, George, 91, 153–7, 163
weaknesses, 20
West Point, *see* United States Military Academy
What, 5, *6*, 7–8
Why, 4–5, *6*, 7–8; *see also* purpose
wicked problems, 129–32, 158–9
Wilderness Trail, 1–2, 28
Wintle, Walter D., 148–9
wisdom, 20–1, 64–7
Woodward, Orrin: *Launching a Leadership Revolution, Mastering the Five Levels of Influence*, 70
World War I, 31
World War II, 121–8, 132, 146
writing, 116

Yoshioka, Seijuro, 57

Ziglar, Zig, 104

"At last, a leadership book written by a real leader." Author Ralph Peters

"Nobody tells a story better than John Antal." Author and analyst
James Jay Carafano

About the Author

John Antal's purpose in life is to "develop leaders and inspire service."
What is your purpose in life?

John is a leadership coach, author, historian, journalist, and speaker. He teaches leadership to private, corporate, government, and military organizations. John served 30 years in the U.S. Army, commanding tank and cavalry units from platoon to brigade and earning the rank of Colonel. After retiring from the U.S. Army, he worked for Microsoft Corporation and then as an Executive Director for an interactive entertainment company working in the U.S. and Canada to create successful, multi-million-dollar AAA+ video game titles. He has appeared on television and radio shows to discuss leadership, historical topics, and national security issues. He writes extensively on these topics and is the author of 16 books and hundreds of magazine articles. John was a member of the United States Army Science Board (ASB) from 2018 to 2021.

You can contact John Antal to teach your team or organization at:
American-Leadership.com.